Samuel Bradhurst Schieffelin

Children of God and Union with Christ

Samuel Bradhurst Schieffelin

Children of God and Union with Christ

ISBN/EAN: 9783337166717

Printed in Europe, USA, Canada, Australia, Japan

Cover: Foto ©Lupo / pixelio.de

More available books at **www.hansebooks.com**

CHILDREN OF GOD

AND

UNION WITH CHRIST

PART I.

BY

SAMUEL B. SCHIEFFELIN

Writer of "The Foundations of History: A Series of First Things;"
"Milk for Babes;" "Children's Bread;" "A Message to
Ruling Elders;" "Words to Christian Teachers;"
"People's Hymn Book," Etc.

WITH A PREFATORY NOTE BY

REV. JOHN HALL, D.D., NEW YORK.

"And this is life eternal, that they may know Thee the only true God and Jesus Christ, whom Thou hast sent."—John 17: 3.

BOARD OF PUBLICATION
OF THE
REFORMED CHURCH IN AMERICA,
25 East 22d Street.
New York

1896

Price, Single Copy, 25 Cents.   By Dozen, 20 Cents Each
Postage, 7 Cents Extra Per Copy.

PREFATORY NOTE.

The "Fatherhood of God" is sometimes used in such a way as to suggest that all human creatures are, in the same sense, His children. Men are often tempted, in view of our nation being called Christian, and of their relation to some Church, to count themselves in the family of God. They overlook the fact that we are a fallen race, and forget that a new birth is needed in order to our being, in the Bible sense of the words, Children of God.

There is crying need for clear convictions on this matter—convictions founded on the inspired word of God. To that word the writer appeals from beginning to end, and that not by collecting detached phrases, but by presenting in their true connection, the full and clear statements of the holy oracles. He has been a life-long student of Scripture, as all who have looked into his many other books well know, and in this volume he brings the Divine light, in a reverent spirit, to the readers' mind on two of the gravest questions that can be raised: Am I a child of God? Is Christ a Saviour whom I can trust, sinner as I am?

There are teachers in our time who credit the blessed Master with all the elements of perfection in His life, and who suggest that men are saved by their appreciating and imitating His purity, benevolence, and other virtues. Such appreciative imitation a true Christian must cultivate, but he must not ignore our Saviour's humiliation, His dying for the sins of His people, and the necessity for union with Him, in order to entrance into the ranks of God's children. Jesus is a matchless teacher, the Prophet sent of God; but He is no less the Great High Priest, through whose offering of Himself a basis is laid, on the ground of which a holy Ruler of the Universe can be just and yet the justifier of a sinner who believes in Jesus and so is in union with Him.

This essential truth is clearly set forth in this volume, in the light in which it stands out in the Old Testament and in the New, for the types and predictions of the one have their realization in the other.

Deeply impressed with the importance of these doctrines, and the need of their being presented to all men, now and at all times, I cannot but wish for this book deep and prayerful study by many. I can vouch for its harmony with scripture, not simply from my knowledge of the writer, but from having read it, and been so impressed by its truthfulness and its timeliness as to ask the privilege of writing these prefatory paragraphs. It will, I trust, be a blessing to many.

JOHN HALL.

INDEX.—Part I.

	PAGE
Introduction	5
All Men are Sinners and are Lost	11
Death and Hell	14
Men cannot find God by their Reason	21
Not Saved by Believing in a Church	24
Union of the Church	28
Sins of the Church before Christ came	32
The Jews	36
Errors in the Church since Christ came	43
The Way of Salvation	60
Special calls of God	71
God commandeth all men everywhere to repent	77
Children of God born again	86
Children of God created anew	90
Children of God made alive from the dead	92
Children of God chosen by Him before the foundation of the world	94
Faith and Good Works	98
The Children of God have everlasting life now	106
The Children of God Witnesses for Christ	110
The Children of God must grow	114

ERRATA.

Page 20—15th line: *You not* should read *You do not*.
Page 47—2d line from bottom: *ovine* should read *wine*.
Page 90—4th line: *in one* should read *in me*.
Page 97—next to bottom line: *in thing* should read *in the thing*.
Page 100—15th line: *delivered from* should read *delivered me from*.
Page 112—last line: *head* should read *heart*.
Page 116—bottom line: *Colasse* should read *Colosse*.
Page 117—12th line: *delivered from* should read *delivered us from*.
Page 120—10th line from bottom: *comfor* should read *comfort*.
Page 159—5th line from bottom: *loyal* should read *royal*.
Page 189—8th line from bottom: *commandeth* should read *commanded*.
Page 191—top line: *me* should read *men*.
Page 202—12th line from bottom: *snd* should read *and*.
Page 223—15th line from bottom: *name* should read *name's*.
Page 226—3d line from bottom: *snall* should read *shall*.
Page 227—9th line from bottom: *spitit* should read *spirit*.
Page 227—5th line from bottom: *heritance* should read *inheritance*.
Page 234—15th line: *incircumcision* should read *uncircumcision*.
Page 235—15th line from top: *father* should read *Father*.
Page 245—16th line: *r.Co* should read *Cor*.
Page 249—4th line: *not forsake* should read *nor forsake*.

INTRODUCTION.

"Ye do err, not knowing the Scriptures" (Matt. 22: 29).

MANY, even of the children of God, think of the Lord Jesus Christ, as having left this world eighteen hundred years ago, and as being now in heaven, as our advocate ; and do not realise "that all power is given unto Him in heaven and in earth" (Matt. 28: 18). "Angels and authorities being made subject unto Him" (1 Pet. 3: 22). "And by Him all things consist. And He is the Head of the body of the Church" (Col. 1: 17) And He is "Far above all principality, and power, and might, and dominion, and every name that is named, not only in this world, but also in that which is to come : and hath put all things under His feet, and gave Him to be the Head of all things to the Church, which is His body, the fulness of Him that filleth all in all" (Eph. 1: 20). They do not realise that the Lord Jesus Christ, omnipotent, omniscient and omnipresent, has been ever since His ascension, and is now, with His Church ; and has a living union with every individual believer in Him. He says, "Where two or three are gathered together in My name, there am I in the midst of them" (Matt. 18 : 20). Few believe this ; if more did, prayer meetings of two or three

Christians meeting in His name, would be more appreciated. "Again, I say unto you, That if two of you shall agree on earth as touching anything that they shall ask, it shall be done for them of My Father that is in heaven" (Matt. 18: 19). "Whatsoever ye shall ask in My name that will I do, that the Father may be glorified in the Son" (John 14: 13). This He repeats again and again (John 15: 7, 16; John 16: 23, 26). Reader, do you believe these promises? He commanded His disciples, "Go ye, therefore, and make disciples of all the nations, and lo, I am with you always, even unto the end of the world" (Matt. 28: 19). "So then, after the Lord had spoken unto them, He was received up into heaven, and sat on the right hand of God. And they went forth, and preached everywhere, the Lord working with them, and confirming the Word with signs following" (Mark 16: 19). If preachers and Christians trying to bring souls to Christ believed this, they would realise His presence with them; and have His Almighty power working with them, confirming the Word. After His ascension, Christ was with the Apostles according to His promise. Where the word Lord appears in the Acts of the Apostles, it refers to the Lord Jesus Christ. "The Lord added to them day by day those that were being saved" (Acts 2: 47). Paul asked, "Who art Thou, Lord? And the Lord said, I am Jesus whom thou persecutest" (Acts 9: 4, 5; 18: 9). In the letters to the churches, in the second and third chapters of the Revelation, we are expressly told that Jesus walks among the churches, and notices all their good works and all their errors in doctrine and practice; and, what should give us great comfort, He knows the trials and troubles of every individual member in every church; and even the poor widow's mite is noticed by Him.

The Bible from the beginning of the first chapter of Genesis, to the end of the last chapter of Revelation, is one Book; and is to be read and studied as one book; as the Word of God; revealing God, through the Lord Jesus Christ. "In the beginning was the Word, and the Word was with God, and the Word was God." "And the Word was made flesh, and dwelt among us" (John 1: 1, 14). The Bible tells us that the Lord Jesus Christ not only was made flesh for us, but also that He takes our sins, and gives us His righteousness. "For He hath made Him to be sin for us, who knew no sin, that we might be made the righteousness of God in Him" (2 Cor. 5: 21). "Who his own self bare our sins in His own body on the tree, that we, being dead to sin should live unto righteousness" (1 Peter 2: 24). He took on Him our death, and gives us His everlasting life. "I give unto them eternal life" (John 10: 28). "Because I live, ye shall live also" (John 14: 19). He took on Him our human nature, and makes us partakers of His Divine nature. "As though father art in Me, and I in Thee, that they, also, may be one in us" (John 17: 21).

It is not surprising that the deluded followers of the Church of Rome are ignorant of the way of salvation. Being forbidden to read the Bible, it is to them a sealed book; but it is a sad fact that many who are connected with Protestant churches, instead of studying the Scriptures, read only such parts as suit them. The consequence is they are ignorant of many of the plain teachings of the Bible; and because of their ignorance of the Bible, they have little faith; and do not possess that joy, and peace, which come through believing. Ask many professing Christians if they believe in the Lord Jesus Christ? And they will without hesitation reply, Yes. Ask them, If you are called away to night, are you sure that you would go to heaven? They will hesitate, and probably reply, I hope so. Ask them, Why they are not sure? They have doubts whether they are good enough. They think it presumption and self-righteousness in those who answer such questions with, Yes, for I have Christ's word for it. They are ignorant of, or do not believe, the words of Christ regarding those who believe in Him. He hath said, "He that believeth on the Son hath everlasting life" (John 3: 36). "Hath everlasting life, and shall not come into condemnation; but is passed from death into life" (John 5: 24). "Verily, verily, I say unto you, he that believeth on Me hath everlasting life"

(John 6 : 47). The Word of God says, "Whosoever believeth that Jesus is the Christ is begotten of God." "He that believeth on the Son of God hath the witness in Him: he that believeth not God hath made Him a liar; because he hath not believed in the witness that God hath borne concerning His Son. And the witness is this, that God gave unto us eternal life, and this life is in His Son. He that hath the Son hath the life; he that hath not the Son of God hath not the life. These things, have I written unto you, that ye may know that ye have eternal life, even unto you that believe on the name of the Son of God" (I John 5: 1, 10).

The following pages are written, that believers in the Lord Jesus Christ may know that they are children of God; having now, everlasting life; and, therefore, they are told, "Grow in the grace and knowledge of our Lord and Saviour Jesus Christ" (II Peter 3 : 18). And they are told how to grow. "As new-born babes, desire the sincere milk of the Word, that ye may grow thereby" (I Peter 2: 2).

Owing to the unfaithfulness of the elders or bishops, many flocks have been scattered and lost. As Paul told the elders of the Church of Ephesus should happen to that church (Acts 20: 28).

There is a lamentable ignorance of the Bible and its plain teachings among professing Christians. Many do not believe what the Bible says about the condition of all men by nature; about the only way of salvation; and that a believer is saved. They do not believe what is written in the following pages. Although nearly all of them are extracts from the Bible. It will be well, for any who may read them, to stop now and then, and ask themselves, Does the Word of God say this? Do I believe it?

ALL MEN ARE SINNERS AND ARE LOST.

"There is none that doeth good, no, not one." Rom. 3: 10.

In the Bible we are told that, "Jehovah looked down from heaven upon the children of men, to see if there were any that did understand, and seek God. They are all gone aside, they are altogether become filthy: there is none that doeth good, no, not one" (Psm. 14: 2). "We are all as an unclean thing, and all our righteousnesses are as filthy rags; and we all do fade as a leaf; and our iniquities, like the wind, have taken us away" (Isai. 64: 6). "The carnal mind is enmity against God: for it is not subject to the law of God, neither indeed can be. So then they that are in the flesh cannot please God" (Rom. 8: 7). "The natural man receiveth not the things of the Spirit of God: for they are foolishness unto him: neither can he know them, because they are spiritually discerned" (1 Cor. 2: 14). "The heart is deceitful above all things, and desperately wicked" (Jer. 17: 10). "From within, out of the heart of men, proceed evil thoughts, adulteries, fornications, murders, thefts, covetousness, wickedness, deceit, lasciviousness, an evil eye, blasphemy, pride, foolishness" (Mark 7: 21). "As it is written, There is none righteous, no, not one: there is none that understandeth, there is none that seeketh after God. They are all gone out of the way, they are together become unprofitable; there is none that doeth good, no, not one" (Rom. 3: 10). "By the deeds of the law there shall no flesh be justified in His sight." "For all have sinned and come short of the glory of God" (Rom. 3: 20, 23). Every man by nature is born a rebel, and continues in rebellion against God until he is converted. As a creature, he owes every instant love and obedience to his Creator. He is adding to his indebtedness to God every moment of his existence. He can never pay any portion of that debt. His only hope is the forgiveness of sin in the way appointed by God, through repentance and faith in the Lord Jesus Christ. "He that believeth not, is condemned already" (John 3: 18). "He that believeth not the Son, shall not see life: but the wrath of God abideth on him" (John 3: 36).

None realise what they were by nature, more than the children of God do, when they are born again. Paul tells the "Saints in Ephesus," "And you hath He quickened, who were dead in trespasses and sins; wherein in time past ye walked according to the course of this world, according to the prince of the power of the air, the spirit that now worketh in the children of disobedience: * * * and were by nature the children of wrath, even as others" (Eph. 2: 1, 3). And Paul, speaking of himself, says, "This is a faithful saying, and worthy of all acceptation, that Christ Jesus came into the world to save sinners; of whom I am chief" (1 Tim. 1: 15). "God commendeth His love toward us, in that, while we were yet sinners, Christ died for us" (Rom. 5: 8). Reader, do you believe what God says is the state of every man by nature? That it is your state; unless you have been convinced of sin by the Holy Spirit, and have been led to repent and to believe in the Lord Jesus Christ?

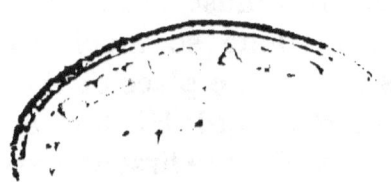

DEATH AND HELL.

"Where their worm dieth not, and the fire is not quenched." Mark 9: 48.

A CENTURY ago, in the churches, men were told of the law of God, and the holiness of God, and the justice of God, to convince them of sin, and to make them feel their need of the Saviour. The church in these days is as the children of Israel were, in the time of Isaiah; "That will not hear the law of the Lord: which say to the seers, See not; and to the prophets, Prophesy not unto us right things, speak unto us smooth things, prophesy deceits" (Isai. 30: 9). The cry now is, You must not preach the terrors of the law of God, you must preach only love. This is now being done so much that humanitarianism is taking the place of the Gospel. God is set aside; His word, His law, and His plan of salvation set aside; the first and great commandment, Thou shalt love the Lord thy God with all thy heart, is put aside; and in their place is preached, You must visit, feed, wash, clothe, educate, and give ethical culture to the masses, to elevate them; and so make them ready to receive the Gospel. They who do this are "ashamed of the Gospel of Christ: for it is the power of God unto salvation" (Rom. 1: 16). All these results in raising man always follow the faithful preaching of the Gospel; and never precede it. This unfaithfulness of the church is not only lulling the world to continue in its false security, but has weakened the faith of many of the children of God; so that many of them are led to doubt what is said in the previous chapter concerning the total depravity of man; and to doubt what the word of God teaches concerning an eternal death and an eternal hell. The reader must bear in mind that the following extracts are from the Word of God. Whether we believe them or not affects our eternal destiny, but cannot alter that word. That word says, "The wages of sin is death; but the gift of God is eternal life through Jesus Christ our Lord" (Rom. 6: 23). "The soul that sinneth, it shall die" (Ezek. 18: 4). The first temptation of the devil was to destroy man's faith in the word of God. "The serpent said unto the woman, Ye shall not surely die" (Gen. 3: 4). Eve believed the devil, and ever since her descendants have been led by him and are his slaves. Adam and Eve by their creation were under the law of God. They were created holy, with the power and the use of a free will. They were put under a particular test of obedience; and charged not to eat of the tree of the knowledge of good and evil; with the penalty of, "in the day thou eatest thereof thou shalt surely die" (Gen. 2: 17). In the original Hebrew it reads, "Dying thou shalt die." An everlasting dying; an **everlasting death.**

The Bible further tells us, "By one man sin entered into the world, and death by sin; and so death passed upon all men, for that all have sinned" (Rom. 5: 12). All past history, and the present state of the world confirm this word of God. Death has passed upon all.

The fearful consequences of continuing in sin, the awful penalty of the everlasting death, dying thou shalt die forever, is not preached as it should be. It was almost the constant theme of John the Baptist, of Christ, and of the Apostles when preaching. John the Baptist aroused all Judea, by calling upon them to escape "The wrath to come" (Matt. 3: 7). A very large portion of the teachings of the Lord Jesus Christ contains the same warnings; and describes in many ways death and hell. For example: "Hell" (Matt. 5: 29, 30; 10: 28). "The damnation of hell" (Matt. 23: 33). "Hell fire" (Matt. 5: 22). "Everlasting fire" (Matt. 18: 8). "Everlasting fire, prepared for the devil and his angels" (Matt. 25: 41). As a place where they are "in torments," separated from others by "a great gulf fixed" (Luke 16: 20, 23, 26). In His description of the last judgment, Jesus said: "In the end of the world the Son of Man shall send forth His angels, and they shall gather out of His kingdom all things that offend, and them which do iniquity; and shall cast them into a furnace of fire: there shall be wailing and gnashing of teeth" (Matt. 13: 40). "Cast ye the unprofitable servant into the outer darkness:

there shall be weeping and gnashing of teeth" (Matt. 25: 30; 8: 12; 22: 13). "So shall it be at the end of the world: the angels shall come forth, and sever the wicked from among the just, and shall cast them into the furnace of fire: there shall be wailing and gnashing of teeth" (Matt. 13. 49; 22: 13). "Into hell, into the fire that never shall be quenched: where their worm dieth not, and the fire is not quenched" (Mark 9: 43, 46, 48). This awful doom is not for those only who are great sinners in the eye of the world, but the servant, who did not employ the one talent committed to him by his lord, received the sentence. "Take therefore the talent from him. . . . And cast ye the unprofitable servant into outer darkness: there shall be weeping and gnashing of teeth" (Matt. 25: 28). We should bear in mind that these words were uttered by Christ, who came, and died, to save men from such a fearful everlasting death. In the description of the Millennium, given in the 20th chapter of the Revelation, when all the kingdoms of this world shall be Christian for a thousand years, we read, His people "shall be priests of God and of Christ, and shall reign with Him a thousand years. And when the thousand years are expired, Satan shall be loosed out of his prison, and shall go out to deceive the nations which are in the four quarters of the earth, Gog and Magog, to gather them together to the war: the number of whom is as the sand of the sea. And they went up over the breadth of the earth, and compassed the camp of the saints about, and the beloved city: and fire came down out of heaven, and devoured them." This falling away after the Millennium, has not received the consideration of those, who insist that Christ is coming personally on the earth to reign a thousand years in Jerusalem, which it should have. Since the day of Pentecost, He has been in closer union with His Church and with every individual believer in Him, than he He could be if bodily present in Jerusalem only. Beside, it cannot be thought, that He is to undergo a second humiliation on the earth, by seeing all nations forsaking Him and shutting Him up with a few saints in Jerusalem. He is on the throne now, and never will be humbled again. The account goes on to describe Hell. "And the Devil that deceived them was cast into the lake of fire and brimstone, where are also the Beast and the false prophet; and they shall be tormented day and night forever and ever. And I saw a great white throne, and Him that sat on it, from whose face the earth and the heaven fled away; and there was found no place for them. And I saw the dead, the great and the small, standing before the throne; and the books were opened; and another book was opened, which is the Book of Life: and the dead were judged out of those things, which were written in the books, according to their works. And the sea gave up the dead which were in it; and death and Hades gave up the dead which were in them: and they were judged according to their works. And death and Hades were cast into the lake of fire. This is the second death, even the lake of fire. And if any was not found written in the Book of Life, he was cast into the lake of fire " (Rev. 20: 6). The sad truth is, that many who profess to believe in the Lord Jesus Christ, through their ignorance of the Scriptures and the weakness of their faith, do not believe these awful truths. The consequence is, they do not appreciate their own salvation; and do not seek, as they should, to save those who are lost. A few years ago, the whole country was interested in the efforts made to save two men who were carried in the rapids above the falls of Niagara to the brink of the falls. They had caught hold of something which kept them from going over. Constant telegrams were sent everywhere giving accounts of the efforts made to save them. After hours of suspense, one could hold on no longer, and was carried over the falls; the other was enabled to cling to a log attached to a rope which had reached them. While being drawn to the bridge, the log struck a rock; he was too weak to hold on to it, was washed off, and was lost. He was almost saved. There is a far more awful descent than over the Falls of Niagara; and a more fearful death, than being carried over them. It is estimated that there is a death every second, or a hundred thousand deaths every day; that thirty-five millions of souls are going into eternity every year. The most of them, "separate from Christ, alienated from the commonwealth of Israel, and strangers from the covenants of the promise, and having no hope and without God in the world" (Eph. 2: 12). The first impulse of the saved is to declare what Christ has done for their souls; the next is, to bring others to Christ. The writer was told of a person's saying, "that he had attended church regularly, and during the last eleven years, he had not heard the word hell mentioned." He was also told, by the son of an elder, "You not believe what is said about hell, nor my father neither; or you would try to save every person you met." "Let this mind be in you, which was also in Christ Jesus, who, being in the form of God, thought it not robbery to be equal with God: but made Himself of no reputation, and took upon Him the form of a servant, and was made in the likeness of men: and being found in fashion as a man, He humbled Himself, and became obedient unto death, even the death of the Cross" (Phil. 2: 5). Jesus said, "The Son of Man is come to seek and to save that which is lost" (Luke 19: 10). "This is a faithful saying, and worthy of all acceptation, that Christ Jesus came into the world to save sinners" (1 Tim. 1: 15). Believer, He did this to save you. Have you the "same mind which was in Christ Jesus?" Are you trying to save others?

MEN CANNOT FIND GOD BY THEIR REASON.

"Neither knoweth any man the Father, save the Son, and he to whomsoever the Son will reveal Him." Matt. 11: 27.

THE first effect of sin in Adam was to make him try to get away from God. "Adam and his wife hid themselves from the presence of the Lord God among the trees of the garden" (Gen. 3: 8). After Cain had murdered Abel, and Jehovah had set a mark upon him, he "went out from the presence of Jehovah, and dwelt in the land of Nod" (Gen. 4: 16). It was well for Adam that God called unto him; otherwise he would have departed farther and farther from God forever. Reason has been a traitor since the fall. Adam and Eve reasoned themselves into sin. "The woman saw that the tree was good for food, and that it was pleasant to the eyes, and a tree to be desired to make one wise, she took of the fruit thereof, and did eat, and gave also unto her husband, and he did eat" (Gen. 3: 6). One effect of the fall was the entire perversion of the reason. Since then man's reason has been controlled by his wicked heart. This is fully described by Paul in the first chapter of the Epistle to the Romans. "For the wrath of God is revealed from heaven against all ungodliness of men, who hold the truth in unrighteousness; because that which may be known of God is manifest in them; for God hath shewed it unto them. For the invisible things of Him from the creation of the world are clearly seen, being understood by the things that are made, even His eternal power and Godhead; so that they are without excuse: because that, when they knew God, they glorified Him not as God, neither were thankful; but became vain in their imaginations, and their foolish heart was darkened. Professing themselves to be wise, they became fools; and changed the glory of the uncorruptible God into an image made like to corruptible man, and to birds, and four-footed beasts, and creeping things. Wherefore God also gave them up to uncleanness, through the lusts of their own hearts, to dishonour their own bodies between themselves. Who changed the truth of God into a lie, and worshipped and served the creature more than the Creator, who is blessed for ever. Amen" (Rom. 1: 18-32).

The Scriptures compare the imparting of the knowledge of God to the natural man to a new creation; making it the same as when light was created by the word of God. Paul says: "But if our gospel be hid, it is hid to them that are lost: in whom the god of this world hath blinded the minds of them which believe not, lest the light of the glorious gospel of Christ, who is the image of God, should shine unto them. For we preach not ourselves, but Christ Jesus the Lord; and ourselves your servants for Jesus' sake. For God, who commanded the light to shine out of darkness, hath shined in our hearts, to give the light of the knowledge of the glory of God in the face of Jesus Christ" (2 Cor. 4: 3). Christ says: "I am the way, the truth, and the life: no man cometh unto the Father but by Me" (John 14: 6). "No man knoweth who the Son is but the Father; and who the Father is but the Son, and he to whom the Son will reveal Him" (Luke 10: 22). Without that knowledge there is no salvation. "No man hath seen God at any time; the only begotten Son, which is in the bosom of the Father, He hath declared Him" (John 1: 18). "Neither is there salvation in any other, for there is none other name given among men whereby we must be saved" (Acts 4: 12). Human reason could not have discovered this way of salvation: it universally rejects it when made known; and would continue to do so unless made willing by the Holy Ghost.

MEN NOT SAVED BY BELIEVING IN A CHURCH.

"In vain do they worship me, teaching for doctrines the commandments of men." (Mark 7: 7).

"Ye reject the commandment of God, that ye may keep your own tradition" (Mark 7: 9).

THE visible Church, during the greater part of the time since its foundation, over three thousand years ago, has been idolatrous and infidel. And the greater part of it at the present time, is Antichrist. Not openly opposing Christ; but putting something in the place of Christ. Substituting their traditions for the Word of God; and exalting the mother of Jesus above Him. They are worshipping the works of their own hands, a wafer, images, relics, etc. With their greater knowledge of the Word of God, they are far greater sinners, and doing far more to oppose Christ, and His Gospel, than the leaders of the Church in the day of Christ; whom He denounces so fearfully; and whom he warns His disciples against. As is recorded in the twenty-third chapter of Matthew, and elsewhere, again, and again, Christ spoke kindly to publicans and sinners, and even to repenting harlots; but His anathemas against false teachers in the Church are most fearful. Believers in the Bible, are in many parts of it warned against false teachers in the Church. "For such are false apostles, deceitful workers, transforming themselves into the Apostles of Christ. And no marvel; for Satan himself is transformed into an angel of light. Therefore it is no great thing if his ministers also be transformed as the ministers of righteousness; whose end shall be according to their works" (2 Cor. 11: 13). The most fearful work of the Devil is his getting control of the Church through its teachers and leaders. Christ speaking of them, says: "Woe unto you, Scribes and Pharisees, hypocrites! for ye shut up the kingdom of heaven against men: for ye neither go in yourselves, neither suffer ye them that are entering to go in" (Matt. 23: 13). The Gospel can be carried to the heathen and they will receive it; but the followers of these false teachers cannot be approached. Forbidden by their priests, they will not listen to the Gospel, and are ready to kill those who bring the Gospel to them. Speaking of the Pharisees, who were offended by His sayings, Christ says, "Let them alone: they be blind leaders of the blind. And if the blind lead the blind, both shall fall into the ditch" (Matt. 15: 14). Speaking of those cities which would not receive the messengers of Christ, Christ said, "It shall be more tolerable for Sodom and Gomorrah in the day of judgment than for them" (Matt. 10: 15; 11: 22, 24; Luke 10: 12–15). While there are some called of God, and saved, even in these lapsed churches, their teachings lead many of their deluded followers to everlasting death. There are some false teachers also, in some of the Protestant Churches; perverting the truth. Their followers, like those described by Isaiah, will not hear the law of God. "Now go, write it before them in a table, and note it in a book, that it may be for the time to come forever and ever: That this is a rebellious people, lying children, children that will not hear of the law of the Lord: which say to the seers, See not; and to the prophets, Prophesy not unto us right things, speak unto us smooth things, prophesy deceits: get you out of the way, turn aside out of the path, cause the Holy One of Israel to cease from among us" (Isaiah 30: 8). "For the time will come when they will not endure sound doctrine; but after their own lusts shall they heap to themselves teachers, having itching ears; and they shall turn away their ears from the truth, and shall be turned unto fables" (2 Tim. 4: 3). "But there were false prophets among the people, even as there shall be false teachers among you, who privily shall bring in damnable heresies, even denying the Lord that bought them, and bring upon themselves swift destruction. And many shall follow their pernicious ways; by reason of whom the way of truth shall be evil spoken of. And through covetousness shall they with feigned words make merchandise of you" (2 Peter 2: 1). Paul tells the saints at Colosse, "Beware, lest any man spoil you, through philosophy and vain deceit, after the tradition of men, after the rudiments of the world, and not after Christ" (Col. 2 : 8). The saints of the present day, need the same warning; that they may not be "spoiled" by the teachings of some ministers and professors in theological seminaries, "which are not after Christ." And also, by " Avoiding profane and vain babblings, and oppositions of science falsely so called ; which some professing have erred concerning the faith " (1 Tim. 6: 20). They who seek to find God, and the way of salvation in any Church or from any ministers, whose teachings are "not after Christ," are lost. What the Bible teaches concerning the errors in doctrine and practice in the churches spoken of in it, will appear in another chapter.

UNION OF THE CHURCH.

"As Thou, Father, art in me, and I in Thee, that they, also, may be one in us" (John 17: 21).

THE cry at the present day for the union of the visible Church is mostly founded on ignorance or on infidelity. It is contrary to the teachings of the Bible, and contrary to the prayer of Christ. The cry is, for all Churches calling themselves Christian to unite; whether they are evangelical, infidel, idolatrous or antichrist; and, that all creeds and confessions must be put aside. This can never be. The true Church may, as has been the case, disappear, or be hidden for a time; but it will, even if only a comparative handful, be kept separate and distinct. It will separate itself from those Churches "which hold the truth in unrighteousness," or put their traditions in the place of the Scriptures. Jesus did this, when He separated His followers from the Church in His day. Christ's prayer for them who believe in Him is, "They might be one, even as He and the Father are one. I in them, and Thou in Me, that they may be made perfect in one;" "That the love wherewith Thou hast loved Me may be in them and I in them" (John 17: 11, 22, 26). The union of believers in the Lord Jesus Christ is not union with a

Church; but is Christ in them, and they in Him. United, they are partakers of the same Spirit ; and thus they are one in Him, and in one another. Believers in Him have always been, and are now, united in Him. His prayer has been answered ever since it was offered.

In almost all ages, the greater part of the visible Church has been opposed to the truth ; and it has been and still is the greatest enemy of Christ and of His followers. Christ, speaking to the leaders and rulers of the visible Church in His day, said, "Woe unto you, Scribes and Pharisees, hypocrites! * * * Ye are the children of them which killed the prophets. Fill ye up then the measure of your fathers. Ye serpents, ye generation of vipers, how can ye escape the damnation of hell? Wherefore, behold I send unto you prophets, and wise men, and scribes: and some of them ye shall kill and crucify ; and some of them shall ye scourge in your synagogues, and persecute them from city to city" (Matt. 23: 29). These words have been literally fulfilled by the visible Church. It crucified Christ; killed, or persecuted them who believed in Him; and for the greater part of the time, ever since, it has continued to do so, wherever it had temporal power ; and in some places it is doing so now. Thus Christ's Word concerning the Church was fulfilled, " That upon you may come all the righteous blood shed upon the earth " (Matt. 23 : 35). The lapsed Churches, generally, hate the truth and them that hold it more than the world does. This was the case before Christ came. It was for this Cain killed Abel. The ten tribes of Israel when they forsook God, became the greatest enemies of the two who remained faithful to His Word and service. Whenever affinity was made with each other, Judah was led into idolatry.

The marriages of the children of God with the children of the world, were followed by the corruption of the entire human race; and was the cause of the Flood sent to destroy all living, excepting those saved in the Ark. In the former dispensation, the children of God were forbidden to form alliances with the idolatrous nations around them; they were forbidden to introduce any of their forms of worship; they were forbidden to join them in worldly business or pursuits; and particularly forbidden to have any marriages between them; "Neither shalt thou make marriages with them, thy daughter thou shalt not give unto his son, nor his daughter shalt thou take unto thy son. For they will turn away thy son from following me, that they may serve other gods" (Deut. 7 : 3). Solomon, the wisest of men, was thus led astray. Such was the fate of Ahab after he married Jezebel. And such now generally follows, when children of Christian parents marry the daughters of lapsed Churches, or of the world. In the New Testament the children of God are told, "Be ye not unequally yoked together with unbelievers: for what fellowship hath righteousness with unrighteousness? And what communion hath light with darkness? And what part hath Christ with Belial? Or what part hath he that believeth with an infidel? And what agreement hath the temple of God with idols? for ye are the temple of the living God; for God hath said, "I will dwell in them; and walk in them; and I will be their God, and they shall be My people" (2 Cor. 6: 14; 1 Cor. 6: 39).

Christ's prayer for believers in Him was, "That they all may be one; as Thou, Father, art in Me, and I in Thee, that they also may be one in us; that the world may believe that Thou hast sent Me. And the glory which Thou gavest Me I have given them; that they may be one, even as we are one; I in them, and thou in Me, that they may be made perfect in one" (John 17: 21). His prayer is answered. His people are one. The union of the Churches, as is proposed, is impossible. If it were possible, the result would be the death of the true Church; and there would be no hope for the world. The twelve tribes of Israel were kept separate; yet they composed one Israel as long as they were faithful to the Word and ordinances of God. When they forsook Him, they were lost.

SINS OF THE CHURCH BEFORE CHRIST CAME.

A VERY large portion of the Old Testament is a record of the sins of the visible church of God. The great wonder is, that God has preserved His word from the beginning to the present day. All men by nature are opposed to it. The rulers of the earth have tried to destroy it. And even the greater part of the church, to whom it was sent, and in whose charge it was, has endeavored to keep it a sealed book away from the people; and has, from age to age, rejected it and put their traditions in the place of it; and it is doing so at the present time. As the church did in the days of Christ; to the rulers of which He said, "Full well ye reject the commandment of God, that ye may keep your own tradition" (Mark 7: 9). "Well hath Esaias prophesied of you hypocrites, as it is written, This people honoureth me with their lips, but their heart is far from me. Howbeit in vain do they worship me, teaching for doctrines the commandments of men" (Mark 7: 6). "Making the word of God of none effect through your tradition" (Mark 7: 13; Matt., chap. 23). In almost every book in the Old Testament we have accounts of the idolatries of the children of Israel, the only church of God in the world.

Immediately after they were delivered from Egypt, and were made God's chosen people, they fashioned with a graven tool a molten calf, and built an altar before it, and they said, "These be thy gods, O Israel, which brought thee up out of the land of Egypt" (Exod, 32: 4). During the four hundred years of the Judges, the various tribes many times fell into idolatry and into captivity. Judges 2: 11-17; 3: 6, 7, 12; 4: 1; 6: 1, 28; 10: 6, etc. After the kingdom was divided, ten of the twelve tribes of Israel worshipped and offered sacrifices to the two calves of gold made by Jeroboam; who had told them, "Behold thy gods, O Israel, which brought thee up out of the land of Egypt" (1 Kings 12: 28). The ten tribes continued their idolatry until they were taken into captivity and lost sight of. The remaining two tribes repeatedly became idolatrous, until they were led into captivity to Babylon. Nearly all of the prophets were sent to the church, to reprove it for forsaking the Lord and His word. Isai. 1: 2; Jer. 1: 18; Ezek. 2: 3; Amos 3; Micah 1: 5, etc. Isaiah, 700 years before Christ, says: "Hear, O heavens, and give ear, O earth: for the Lord hath spoken; I have nourished and brought up children, and they have rebelled against me. The ox knoweth his owner, and the ass his master's crib: but Israel doth not know, my people doth not consider. Ah sinful nation, a people laden with iniquity, a seed of evil doers, children that are corrupters: they have forsaken the Lord, they have provoked the Holy One of Israel unto anger, they are gone away backward." * * * "Bring no more vain oblations; incense is an abomination unto me, the new moons and Sabbaths, the calling of assemblies, I cannot away with, it is iniquity, even the solemn meeting. Your new moons and your appointed feasts my soul hateth: they are a trouble to me; I am weary to bear them. And when ye spread forth your hands, I will hide mine eyes from you; yea, when ye make many prayers, I will not hear: your hands are full of blood" (Isai. 1: 2, 13). "His watchmen are blind: they are all ignorant, they are all dumb dogs, they cannot bark; sleeping, lying down, loving to slumber. Yea, they are greedy dogs which can never have enough, and they are shepherds that cannot understand: they all look to their own way, every one for his gain, from his quarter" (Isai. 56: 10). A great part of the book of Jeremiah, 600 years before Christ, consists of accusations against the church in his day, and denounces the judgments of God upon them for their idolatries. Jer. 1: 14, 16; 2: 8. "The prophets prophesy falsely, and the priests bear rule by their means; and my people love to have it so" (Jer. 5: 31). The prophet Ezekiel is sent by the Lord to deliver the same messages to Israel, "And he said unto me, Son of man, I send thee to the children of Israel, to a rebellious nation that hath rebelled against me: they and their fathers have transgressed against Me, even unto this very day. For they are impudent children and stiff-hearted. I do send thee unto them; and thou shalt say unto them, Thus saith the Lord God" (Ezek. 2: 3). "And he said unto me, Son of man, go, get thee unto the house of Israel, and speak my words unto them. * * * But the house of Israel will not hearken unto thee; for they will not hearken unto me" (Ezek. 3: 4–7). "Her priests have violated my law." "Her prophets have daubed them with untempered mortar, seeing vanity, and divining lies unto them, saying, Thus saith the Lord God, when the Lord hath not spoken" (Ezek. 22: 26, 28). The accusations made against the ancient church are applicable to the greater part of the church of the present day.

THE JEWS.

Since God called Abraham, nearly four thousand years ago, his descendants through Isaac and Jacob have been God's chosen people. Their preservation to the present day has been a perpetual miracle. For nearly two thousand years before Christ came, they were the only people of God in the world. His visible church; chosen, delivered, guided, protected by Him; and possessing His word. All the messages of God to the human race; all the revelations of God; of Himself, of His law, of His plan of salvation, were made to the Jews. All the writers of the Bible, the Old Testament and the New, all the prophets, all the apostles, were Jews. And Christ Himself was a Jew. As Christ said to the woman of Samaria, "Salvation is of the Jews" (John 4: 22).

While the children of Israel were yet in the wilderness, before they entered into the promised land, Moses told them of the blessings which would come upon them if they obeyed the Lord, and of the curses which should come upon them, if they did not observe all His commandments and statutes. He said unto them : "Cursed shalt thou be in the city, and cursed shalt thou be in the field. Cursed shall be thy basket and thy store. Cursed shall be the fruit of thy body, and the fruit of thy land, the increase of thy kine, and the flocks of thy sheep. Cursed shalt thou be when thou comest in, and cursed shalt thou be when thou goest out" (Deut. 28: 15). After specifying many other judgments that the Lord should send upon them, he says: "And thou shalt become an astonishment, a proverb, and a by-word, among all nations whither the LORD shall lead thee." * * * "And the LORD shall scatter thee among all people, from one end of the earth even unto the other; and there thou shalt serve other gods, which neither thou nor thy fathers have known, even wood and stone. And among these nations shalt thou find no ease, neither shall the sole of thy foot have rest" (Deut. 28: 37, 64). Six hundred years before Christ came, Jeremiah wrote, "And I will deliver them to be removed into all the kingdoms of the earth for their hurt, to be a reproach and a proverb, a taunt and a curse, in all places whither I shall drive them" (Jer. 24: 9). "And I will persecute them with the sword, with the famine, and with the pestilence, and will deliver them to be removed to all the kingdoms of the earth, to be a curse, and an astonishment, and a hissing, among all the nations whither I have driven them; because they have not hearkened to My words, saith the LORD, which I sent unto them by My servants the prophets, rising up early and sending them; but ye would not hear, saith the Lord" (Jer. 29: 18). The Lord then adds,

"I am with thee, saith the Lord, to save thee : though I make a full end of all nations, whither I have scattered thee, yet will I not make a full end of thee; but I will correct thee in measure, and will not leave thee altogether unpunished" (Jer. 30 : 11 ; 46 : 28). In accordance with His Word, God has been making a "full end of all nations whither I have scattered thee, yet will I not make a full end of thee."

The nations that made captives of the Jews have passed away: and the prophecies concerning them have been literally fulfilled. "Babylon, the glory of kingdoms, the beauty of the Chaldees' excellency, shall be as when God overthrows Sodom and Gomorrah. It shall never be inhabited, neither shall it be dwelt in from generation to generation" (Isa. 13: 19; 14: 22, 47). Nineveh described as much larger than Babylon, after suffering the judgments of God; the angel of the Lord having in one night destroyed "a hundred and four score and five thousand" (Isa. 37 : 36). "Nineveh is laid waste" (Nahum 3: 7). The destruction of Babylon and Nineveh and the state in which their ruins have continued, according to prophecy, is more wonderful than their first growth and grandeur. For more than two thousand years, the prophecies in the Word of God concerning Egypt have been fulfilling. During all that time Egypt has been as she is now, "without a native prince," and "the basest of kingdoms" (Ezek. 29 : 15 ; 30 : 13). The prophecies also against the nations that hated the Jews, when they represented the Church of God, and who rejoiced in the destruction of Jerusalem, God, according to His Word, has made a full end of; they have disappeared from the earth. To the Ammonites: "Thus saith the Lord God; because thou has clapped thine hands, and stamped with the feet, and rejoiced in heart with all thy despite against the land of Israel; behold, therefore, I will stretch out mine hand upon thee, and will deliver thee to the heathen; and I will cut thee off from the people, and I will cause thee to perish out of the countries: I will destroy thee; and thou shalt know that I am the Lord" (Ezek. 25 : 6). For the same reason God said: "I will execute judgments on Moab" (Ezek. 25 : 14). "I will lay my vengeance upon Edom." "For thy violence against thy brother Jacob shame shall cover thee, and thou shalt be cut off forever." There is none "remaining of the house of Esau" "The things of Esau" have been "so searched out, and his hidden things sought up," that not a relic can be found in their ancient dwellings. (Obad 18; Jer. 49: 17; Ezek. 25: 13). For the same cause, judgments were to be executed on the Philistines; and also upon Tyre; then one of the richest cities in the world. "They shall destroy the walls of Tyrus, and break down her towers: I will also scrape her dust from her, and make her like the top of a rock. It shall be a place for the spreading of nets in the midst of the sea" (Ezek. 26: 2). These prophecies have been literally fulfilled.

"Behold, the days come, saith the Lord, that I will make a new covenant with the house of Israel, and with the house of Judah: not according to the covenant that I made with their fathers, in the day that I took them by the hand to bring them out of the land of Egypt; which My covenant they brake, although I was a husband unto them, saith the LORD: but this shall be the covenant that I will make with the house of Israel: After those days, saith the Lord, I will put My law in their inward parts, and write it in their hearts; and will be their God, and they shall be My people. And they shall teach no more every man his neighbor, and every man his brother, saying, Know the LORD: for they shall all know Me, from the least of them, unto the greatest of them, saith the LORD" (Jer. 31: 31). "A new heart also will I give you, and a new spirit will I put within you: and I will take away the stony heart out of your flesh, and I will give you a heart of flesh. And I will put My spirit within you, and cause you to walk in My statutes." * * * "Thus saith the Lord God: I will yet for this be inquired of by the house of Israel, to do it for them" (Ezek. 36: 19, 24, 25, 26, 37). Two hundred years before Jeremiah, Amos prophesied: "Behold, the eyes of the Lord God are upon the sinful kingdom, and I will destroy it from off the face of the earth; saving that I will not utterly destroy the house of Jacob, saith the LORD. For, lo, I will command, and I will sift the house of Israel among all nations, like as corn is sifted in a sieve, yet shall not the least grain fall upon the earth " (Amos 9: 8). Christ said : "And they shall fall by the edge of the sword, and shall be led away captive into all nations : and Jerusalem shall be trodden down of the Gentiles, until the times of the Gentiles be fulfilled " (Luke 21: 24). Paul says : "I say then, Have they stumbled that they should fall ? God forbid: but rather through their fall salvation is come unto the Gentiles." * * * "For if the casting away of them be the reconciling of the world, what shall the receiving of them be, but life from the dead." * * * " For I would not, brethren, that ye should be ignorant of this mystery, lest ye should be wise in your own conceits; that blindness in part is happened to Israel, until the fulness of the Gentiles be come in. And so all Israel shall be saved " (Rom. 11 : 11, 15, 25).

Since their return from their captivity in Babylon, five hundred years before Christ came to the present day, the Jews have never been idolaters; but have remained faithful to the worship of one God; while for over twelve hundred years, the whole visible Christian Church was grossly idolatrous. They are living witnesses for the truth of the writings of Moses and of the prophets ; of the truthfulness of the whole Bible; although for two thousand years, all men have been against them. The wonderful prophecies concerning their dispersion have been literally fulfilled; and are being so now; and the prophecies of their being brought again into the visible Church, with the fulness of the Gentiles, are equally certain. A full end has God made, according to His Word, of many nations: but the Jews, although without a country, and sifted through all nations, still continue a great people; witnesses for the truth of the Bible, as they have been in all the past generations; and they will continue a perpetual miracle, proving the truth of the Word of God to the generations to come; until the Gospel shall be preached to all nations; and then, shall the Jews be brought into the Church of Christ; with the fulness of the Gentiles (Rom. 11: 25).

ERRORS IN CHURCHES SINCE CHRIST CAME.

In the New Testament we have the account of the Church in the days of Christ. In the Epistles, we have a record of the errors in the churches founded by the Apostles. In the Revelation, we have the errors of the seven churches in Asia, which led to the removal of their light, and to their extinction; and also, a prophetic account of the rise and fall of the great apostate church. The most of the errors, spoken of and condemned, still exist in the greater part of the churches. The children of God should be warned against them; that they may avoid them. In the Gospels, we read the warnings of Christ against the rulers of the Church in His day. "Take heed and beware of the leaven of the Pharisees and of the Sadducees" (Matt. 16: 6). "They be blind leaders of the blind" (Matt. 15: 14). "Thus have ye made the commandment of God of none effect by your tradition" (Matt. 15: 6). "Ye serpents, ye generation of vipers, how can ye escape the the damnation of hell?" (Matt. 23: 33). The "generation of vipers" still lives; and they are the leaders in large portions of the Church at the present day. It was to a ruler in the Church, Christ said: "Except a man be born again, he cannot see the kingdom of God" (John 3: 3, 5). It was to the leaders in the Church that Jesus said: "Ye neither know Me, nor My Father: if ye had known Me, ye would have known My Father also" (John 8: 19). The greater part of the Church has had such teachers and rulers ever since. The account Christ gives of their teachings and works, as recorded in the twenty-third chapter of Matthew and elsewhere, should be studied: and believers in Christ should take heed and beware of them. In the Epistle to the Corinthians Paul writes: "It hath been declared unto me of you, my brethren, by them of the house of Chloe, that there are contentions among you. Now this I say, that every one of you saith, I am of Paul; and I of Apollos; and I of Cephas; and I of Christ. Is Christ divided? Was Paul crucified for you? (1 Cor. 1: 11). There would be fewer contentions in the Church, if men had regard to the words of Christ, instead of following men. In the fifth chapter he charges them with not using proper discipline over the members of their church. "It is reported commonly that there is fornication among you." And tells them, "A little leaven leaveneth the whole lump. Purge out, therefore, the old leaven" (1 Cor. 5: 1, 5, 7). "Now, therefore, there is utterly a fault among you, because ye go to law one with another" (1 Cor. 6: 1–7). "I hear that there be divisions among you; and I partly believe it For there must be also heresies among you, that they which are approved may be manifest among you" (1 Cor. 11: 18). "When ye come together therefore into one place, this is not to eat the Lord's Supper. For in eating every one taketh before other his own supper; and one is hungry, and another is drunken. * * * Shall I praise you in this? I praise you not" (1 Cor. 11: 20). "I fear, lest when I come, I shall not find you such as I would, and that I shall be found unto you such as ye would not: lest there be debates, envyings, wraths, strifes, backbitings, whisperings, swellings, tumults" (2 Cor. 12: 20). To the churches of Galatia, he writes: "I marvel that ye are so soon removed from him that called you into the grace of Christ unto another Gospel which is not another; but there be some that trouble you, and would pervert the Gospel of Christ" (Gal. 1: 6). "When Peter was come to Antioch, I withstood him to the face, because he was to be blamed." * * * "And the other Jews dissembled likewise with him; insomuch that Barnabas also was carried away with their dissimulation. But when I saw that they walked not uprightly according to the truth of the Gospel, I said unto Peter before them all, etc." (Gal. 2: 11). Continuing, Paul writes, "O foolish Galatians, who hath bewitched you, that ye should not obey the truth" (Gal. 3: 1). "Are ye so foolish? having begun in the Spirit, are ye now made perfect by the flesh?" (Gal. 3: 3). "How turn ye again to the weak and beggarly elements, whereunto ye desire again to be in bondage? Ye observe days, and months, and times, and years. I am afraid of you, lest I have bestowed upon you labor in vain" (Gal. 4: 9). To the saints at Philippi, he writes: "For many walk, of whom I have told you often, and now tell you even weeping, that they are the enemies of the cross of Christ" (Phil. 3: 18). To the saints in Colosse, he writes: "Beware lest any man spoil you through philosophy and vain deceit after the tradition of men, after the rudiments of the world, and not after Christ" (Col. 2: 8). "Let no man therefore judge you in meat, or in drink, or in respect of an holy day, or of the new moon, or of the Sabbath days: which are a shadow of things to come; but the body is of Christ. Let no man beguile you of your reward in a voluntary humility and worshipping of angels, intruding into those things which he hath not seen, vainly puffed up by his fleshly mind. * * * (Touch not; taste not; handle not; which all are to perish with the using); after the commandments and doctrines of men. Which things have indeed a shew of wisdom in will worship, and humility, and neglecting of the body; not in any honour to the satisfying of the flesh" (Col. 2: 16–23). Paul wrote to the saints in Rome, "The kingdom of God is not meat and drink; but righteousness, and peace, and joy in the Holy Ghost" (Rom. 14: 17). To the Church in Corinth, he writes: "Meat commendeth us not to God: for neither, if we eat, are we the better; neither if we eat not, are we the worse" (1 Cor. 8: 8). He warns them lest they become a stumbling-block to them that are weak, not to eat those things which are offered to idols" (1 Cor. 8: 9). He warns the Church of the Thessalonians, "That ye be not soon shaken in mind, or be troubled, neither by spirit, nor by word, nor by letter as from us, as that the day of Christ is at hand. Let no man deceive you by any means: for that day shall not come, except there come a falling away first, and that man of sin be revealed, the son of perdition; who opposeth and exalteth himself above all that is called God, or that is worshipped; so that he as God sitteth in the temple of God, shewing himself that he is God" (2 Thess. 2: 2). To Timothy Paul writes: Now the Spirit speaketh expressly, that in latter times some shall depart from the faith, giving heed to seducing spirits, and doctrines of devils; speaking lies in hypocrisy; having their conscience seared with a hot iron; forbidding to marry, and commanding to abstain from meats" (1 Tim. 4: 1). A more full description of that great apostacy is given in the seventeenth and eighteenth chapters of the Revelation, where the idolatrous church is described as "the great whore that sitteth upon many waters: with whom the kings of the earth have committed fornication, and the inhabitants of the earth have been made drunk with the ovine of her fornication. * * * Drunken with the blood of the saints, and with the blood of the martyrs of Jesus. * * * And he said: The waters which thou sawest, where the whore sitteth, are peoples, and multitudes, and nations and tongues. * * * And the woman which thou sawest is that great city, which reigneth over the kings of the earth" (Rev. 17: 1-18). That city was Rome. Those prophecies have been fulfilled in the past history and present doings of the Church of Rome. The prediction of its coming destruction we have in the eighteenth chapter of Revelation. In the second and third chapters of the Revelation, we have an account of the errors in the seven churches in Asia; which it would be well for believers in Christ, and particularly the elders of the churches at the present day to study, that they may avoid those errors; and keep the churches now existing, some of which have the same errors in doctrine and practice, from the same destruction. The letter of Christ to the Church of Ephesus, then one of the grandest cities in the world, is peculiarly instructive. The description of that church is such, that it might have been supposed it would have been preserved as a model. It lacked, however, one thing. "I know thy works, and thy labors, and thy patience, and how thou canst not bear them which are evil; and thou hast tried them which say they are apostles, and are not, and hast found them liars; and hast borne, and hast patience, and for My name's sake hast labored and hast not fainted. Nevertheless, I have somewhat against thee, because thou hast left thy first love. Remember, therefore, from whence thou art fallen, and repent, and do the first works, or else I will come unto thee quickly, and will remove thy candlestick out of his place, except thou repent" (Rev. 2: 1). The elders of the Church of Ephesus had previously been warned by the Apostle Paul. We are told that "from Miletus he sent to Ephesus, and called the elders of the church. And when they were come unto him, he said unto them." * * * Take heed therefore unto yourselves, and to all the flock, over the which the Holy Ghost hath made you overseers (R. V. bishops), to feed the Church of God, which He hath purchased with His own blood. For I know this, that after my departing shall grievous wolves enter in among you, not sparing the flock. Also of your own selves shall men arise, speaking perverse things, to draw away disciples after them" (Acts 20: 17, 28). Both predictions have been fulfilled. The Church of Ephesus has been blotted out of existence. And Ephesus itself with its great temple of Diana, has disappeared, leaving only a few ruins. If the elders or bishops of that church had followed Paul's advice and continued faithful, the church and the city might probably have been preserved. Ten righteous men would have saved Sodom.

In all ages the danger has not been from the

world, but from the visible Church becoming apostate and antichrist. At the present time, there are churches claiming that they are the only true Church, saying that they have an "Historical Episcopate," direct successors of the Apostles. The churches that make these claims have not a single church officer, bishop, priest or deacon, or a single congregation in the world such as were the officers appointed, and the congregations or churches formed by the Apostles. Any person taking the word Apostle, Bishop, Priest, Deacon as found in the New Testament, will readily see this. The first chapter of the Acts shows the qualifications necessary for a person to be chosen a successor of an Apostle. "Of these men which have companied with us all the time that the Lord Jesus went in and out among us, beginning from the baptism of John, unto that same day that He was taken up from us, must one be ordained to be a witness with us of His resurrection. * * * And the lot fell upon Matthias; and he was numbered with the eleven Apostles" (Acts 1: 21). Since that day no one has had the qualifications necessary to be called a "successor of the Apostles." Paul was especially called by Christ to be an Apostle. He says: "Am I not an Apostle? Am I not free? Have I not seen Jesus Christ our Lord?" (1 Cor. 9: 1). "After that He was seen of James; then of all the Apostles. And last of all He was seen of me also, as of one born out of due time, for I am the least of the Apostles" (1 Cor. 15: 7). The believer in the Bible may well be warned against "false apostles, deceitful workers, transforming themselves into the Apostles of Christ" (2 Cor. 11: 13). There was no special order of priests in the churches formed by the Apostles. The word priest does not occur in the New Testament in connection with the Christian ministry. The New Testament declares that all believers are now priests. Peter, writing to believers "scattered throughout Pontus, Galatia, Cappadocia, Asia and Bithynia," tells them "Ye are a chosen generation, a royal priesthood, a holy nation, a peculiar people; that ye should shew forth the praises of Him who hath called you out of darkness into His marvellous light" (1 Peter 1: 1; 2: 9). The praise of the redeemed to Jesus Christ in heaven is "Unto Him that loved us, and washed us from our sins in His own blood, and hath made us kings and priests, unto God and His Father; to Him be glory and dominion forever and ever" (Rev. 1: 5). "And they sing a new song, saying: Thou art worthy to take the book, and to open the seals thereof; for Thou wast slain, and hast redeemed us to God by Thy blood out of every kindred, and tongue, and people, and nation ; and hast made us unto our God kings and priests; and we shall reign on the earth " (Rev. 5: 9; 20: 6). The believer in the Bible should beware of those making claims to be priests, as a special order in the Church. There was no such order in the churches founded by the Apostles. Priestcraft has brought untold evil into the Church and into the world. In the sixth chapter of the Acts we have the foundation of the order of Deacons. They were chosen simply to attend to the wants of the poor and needy in the Church. (Acts 6; Phil. 1: 1; I Tim. 3: 8). The most important office in the Church in all ages, as rulers and teachers, is the office of elder. An office entirely ignored by the greater part of the visible Church. If every congregation of believers had been organized as was directed by the Word of God, with elders as overseers or bishops, and if they had been faithful to the duties connected with the office, the churches mentioned in the New Testament, all of which have disappeared, would still have been lights in the world. The Church would not have apostatized and been for so long a period antichrist. In all ages since the Church was founded, elders were appointed to rule. In most of the time since its foundation the elders have not been faithful; and the flocks have been scattered or destroyed. Many who have received the title of doctors of divinity from colleges, which may be infidel, and have no right to confer such titles; are like the watchmen in the days of Isaiah. " His watchmen are blind; they are all ignorant; they are all dumb dogs, they cannot bark" (Isa. 56: 10). The Word of the Lord to Ezekiel was: "So thou, O, son of man, I have set thee a watchman unto the house of Israel ; therefore thou shalt hear the Word at My mouth, and warn them from Me. When I say unto the wicked man, thou shalt surely die; if thou dost not speak to warn the wicked from his way, that wicked man shall die in his iniquity; but his blood will I require at thine hand" (Ezek. 33: 7). The Apostles, as they gathered congregations of believers, had chosen men ordained over each one of them, as elders, overseers or bishops. All these words are used in the New Testament to represent the same office. As it is written, "And when they had ordained elders in every church" (Acts 14: 23). "And the Apostles and Elders came together for to consider of this matter" (Acts 15: 6) "They delivered them the decrees for to keep, that were ordained by the Apostles and Elders which were at Jerusalem" (Acts 16: 6). "And from Miletus he sent to Ephesus, and called the elders of the church." And in his charge he tells them, "Take heed, therefore, unto yourselves, and to all the flock over which the Holy Ghost hath made you overseers (Rev. Ver. bishops)" (Acts 20: 17, 28). In his letter to the congregation at Philippi, he addresses it: "To all the saints in Christ Jesus which are at Philippi, with the bishops and deacons" (Phil. 1: 1). In the epistle to Titus, he writes: "For this cause I left thee in Crete, that thou shouldest set in order the things that are wanting, and ordain elders in every city; as I had appointed thee. If any be blameless, the husband of one wife, having faithful children not accused of riot, or unruly. For a bishop must be blameless, as the steward of God. * * * Holding fast the faithful Word as he has been taught, that he may be able by sound doctrine both to exhort and to convince the gainsayers" (Titus 1: 5-10). According to this, no congregation of believers, is "set in order," without having elders ordained over it. In the Epistle to Timothy, directions are given relating to bishops and deacons. (1 Tim. 3: 1-10; 5: 1, 19). The elders were appointed to rule and also to labor in the Word and doctrine. "Let the elders that rule well be counted worthy of double honor, especially they who labor in the Word and doctrine" (1 Tim. 5: 17). In his first Epistle, Peter writes: "The elders which are among you I exhort, who am also an elder, and a witness of the sufferings of Christ, and also a partaker of the glory that shall be revealed. Feed the flock of God which is among you, taking the oversight thereof, not by constraint, but willingly; not for filthy lucre, but of a ready mind; neither as being lords over God's heritage, but being ensamples to the flock" (1 Peter 5: 1).

In the old dispensation, the priests, the sacrifices, the altar, and the temple were types which were done away with when they were fulfilled when Christ came. Most of the great cathedrals in the world in all countries were erected by an idolatrous Church; and have been hotbeds of priestcraft, ignorance of the Scriptures, of the way of salvation, and of the grossest idolatry. Instead of building new ones, it would be a great benefit if they were all swept from the face of the earth. "For thus saith the high and lofty One that inhabiteth eternity, whose name is Holy; I dwell in the high and holy place, with him also that is of a contrite spirit, to revive the spirit of the humble, and to revive the heart of the contrite ones" (Isa. 57: 15). "Thus saith the Lord: The heaven is My throne, and the earth is My footstool: where is the house that ye build unto Me? And where is the place of My rest? For all these things hath Mine hand made, and all those things have been, saith the Lord: but to this man will I look, even to him that is poor and of a contrite spirit, and trembleth at My Word" (Isa. 66: 1). The children of God are now the Temple of God. "Know ye not that ye are the Temple of God, and that the Spirit of God dwelleth in you" (1 Cor. 3: 16). "For ye are the Temple of the living God; as God hath said, I dwell in them, and walk in them" (2 Cor. 6: 16; Eph. 2: 21, 22).

The word altar does not appear in the New Testament, except when referring to its use in the old, sacrifices being done away with, there is no more use for altars in the churches. Sacrifices being types of the sacrifice of Christ, are all done away with. "For now once at the end of the ages hath He been manifested to put away sin by the sacrifice of Himself" (Heb. 9: 25-28). "Sacrifices and offerings and whole burnt offerings and sacrifices for sin thou wouldst not, neither hadst pleasure therein (the which are offered according to the law), then hath He said, Lo, I am come to do Thy will. He taketh away the first, that He may establish the second. By which will we have been sanctified through the offering of the body of Jesus Christ once for all. And every priest indeed standeth day by day ministering and offering oftentimes the same sacrifices, the which can never take away sins: but He when He had offered one sacrifice for sins forever, sat down on the right hand of God; from henceforth expecting till His enemies be made the footstool of His feet. For by one offering He hath perfected forever them that are sanctified" (Heb. 10: 8). The Passover continued to be a memorial of the deliverance from Egypt in the Church until Christ was offered as a sacrifice. It was a memorial, a type of the Lord's Supper, and was done away with when Christ was crucified. It was at the last celebration of the Passover, that Jesus said, "With desire I have desired to eat this Passover with you before I suffer : for I say unto you, I will not eat it, until it be fulfilled in the kingdom of God" (Luke 22: 15). "Our Passover also hath been sacrificed, even Christ" (1 Cor. 5: 7). As the Passover was a memorial, so is the Lord's Supper. Christ said, "This do in remembrance of Me" (Luke 22: 19).

In the account given 1 Cor. 11: 23 of the Sacrament, it is described as a memorial. "For as often as ye eat this bread, and drink the cup, ye proclaim the Lord's death till He come." They who profess to turn the bread or wafer into the body of Christ and worship it, are guilty of perversion of the Scriptures, of blasphemy and idolatry. The sacrifices which Christians are to offer are themselves and their gifts. "I beseech you therefore, brethren, by the mercies of God, to present your bodies a living sacrifice, holy, acceptable to God, which is your reasonable service" (Rev. Ver. Margin, Spiritual Worship). (Rom. 12: 1). Paul writes: "I am filled, having received from Epaphroditus the things that came from you, an odour of a sweet smell, a sacrifice acceptable, well pleasing to God" (Phil. 4: 18).

The Church which claims to be "The Church," and that it has "the Historical Episcopacy," is bearing its proper fruit. Its historical episcopacy being insisted upon; its ritual, with the doctrines of baptismal regeneration, its altar and priesthood, continually kept in the foreground, has been leading that Church rapidly backward toward Rome. The number of the churches is increasing at a fearful rate in Great Britain, where prayers for the dead are offered, incense is used, the confessional established, the consecrated water elevated and reserved, transubstantiation is taught, and there seems nothing to separate its clergy from that of Rome, but the refusal to acknowledge the primacy of the Pope, and accept the celibacy of the clergy. These are the inevitable results of the teachings of all the Churches that put their traditions in the place of the Word of God.

The Reformed Church of Holland was started with the soundest of creeds and with elders according to the Scriptures. The neglect of the elders allowed the State to appoint heretical teachers in her theological schools to train ministers for her churches. These corrupted nearly the whole Church. The churches in New England not being formed with elders according to the Scriptures, allowed the introduction of heresies, universalism and unitarianism, etc.; which carried a great part of them into infidelity. The neglect of the elders in the Presbyterian Church in controlling some of its theological seminaries, has allowed the entrance of errors which have caused much evil and trouble in that branch of the Church.

If the elders of the Churches were faithful in seeing that their ministers, evangelists and teachers preached the Law of God, the wrath to come, and the Gospel, as Christ and the Apostles preached them, there would be fewer murders, less suicides, less crime and more souls saved. It is written of the Bereans: "These were more noble than those in Thessalonica, in that they received the Word with all readiness of mind, and searched the Scriptures daily, whether those things were so" (Acts 17: 11).

Believers must try the teachings of their Church by the Scriptures. The elders of the Churches are bound to take heed to the flocks over the which the Holy Ghost hath made them bishops, to keep them from being scattered or destroyed.

THE WAY OF SALVATION.

THE Bible tells us, that there is only one way of salvation. That way has been provided by God. Man never would have discovered it; and man everywhere rejects it. That way was the same before Christ came, that it is now. It is the only way in which man can go to God. In that way God's law is honored, and His justice satisfied; the sins of the believer are atoned for; and the sinner is not only justified, but is also sanctified. His natural heart is changed, he is created anew. Man is condemned to death, and "without shedding of blood there is no remission" (Heb. 9: 22). Christ was "made sin for us" (2 Cor. 5: 21), and "bore our sins in his own body on the tree" (1 Pet. 2: 24). The sacrifices offered by the patriarchs, and according to the laws of Moses, were all ordered by God, and were types of the sacrifice of Christ. "The Lamb of God slain from the foundation of the world" (Rev. 13: 8). The coming of Christ was announced immediately after the Fall. "The Lord God said unto the serpent, * * * And I will put enmity between thee and the woman, and between thy seed and her seed; it shall bruise thy head, and thou shalt bruise his heel" (Gen.

3: 15). This enmity has shown itself to the present day. "The children of God are manifest, and the children of the devil" (1 John 3: 10). "Cain, who was of that wicked one, and slew his brother, and wherefore slew he him? Because his own works were evil, and his brother's righteous" (1 John 3: 12). Jesus told the rulers of the church in His day, "Ye are of your father the devil, and the lusts of your father ye will do. He was a murderer from the beginning, and abode not in the truth" (John 8: 44). John the Baptist, before, had addressed them, "O generation of vipers" (Matt. 3: 7). Jesus uses the same words, Matt. 12: 34; and again, "Ye serpents, ye generation of vipers, how can ye escape the damnation of hell?" (Matt. 23: 33). Believers in the Bible must bear in mind that these words were used against the rulers of the church. The seed of the serpent still bears rule in portions of the church, opposing Christ and His teachings. "By faith Abel offered unto God a more excellent sacrifice than Cain" (Heb. 11: 4). Faith in the Lamb slain, which God had provided. Christ was again made known in the promise made to Abraham, "In thee shall all the families of the earth be blessed" (Gen. 12: 3). Jesus said, "Your father, Abraham, rejoiced to see My day; and he saw it, and was glad" (John 8: 56). Job said, "I know that my Redeemer liveth, and that He shall stand up at the last upon the earth" (Job 19: 25). All the forms of worship ordered by God, through Moses, were types of Christ. Access to God, the forgiveness of sins, and His blessing, being all obtained through the appointed sacrifices. In the Psalms we have the gospel and its effects upon believers. "Blessed is he whose transgression is forgiven, whose sin is covered. Blessed is the man unto whom the Lord imputeth not iniquity" (Psm. 32: 1). "Jehovah is my Shepherd, I shall not want" (Psm. 23). "Bless the Lord, O my soul: and all that is within me bless His holy name * * * who forgiveth all thine iniquities; who healeth all thy diseases; who redeemeth thy life from destruction. * * * As far as the east is from the west, so far hath He removed our transgressions from us" (Psm. 103: 1, 3, 12; Psm. 91, etc., etc.). Christ is clearly revealed in the 53rd chapter of Isaiah. "Surely He hath borne our griefs, and carried our sorrows: yet we did esteem Him stricken, smitten of God, and afflicted. But He was wounded for our transgressions, He was bruised for our iniquities; the chastisement of our peace was upon Him; and with His stripes we are healed. All we, like sheep, have gone astray; we have turned every one to his own way; and the LORD had laid on him the iniquity of us all." The whole chapter is full of the Gospel. Christ, after his resurrection, said, "These are the words which I spake unto you, while I was yet with you, that all things must be fulfilled, which were written in the law of Moses, and in the

Prophets, and in the Psalms, concerning me" (Luke 24: 27, 44).

Much of what is done in the cities at the present time, under the pretence of drawing men to hear the Gospel, degrades the message of God, and is insulting God. He sends His ambassadors to preach the Gospel and to beseech men to be reconciled to Him. His message is, Repent and believe in the Lord Jesus Christ. This message is to be delivered to all; whether rich or poor, learned or ignorant; whether in the church or out of it. Unless they repent and believe, they will all likewise perish. The message is, "God so loved the world, that He gave His only begotten Son, that whosoever believeth in Him should not perish, but have everlasting life. For God sent not His Son into the world to condemn the world; but that the world through Him, might be saved" (John 3: 16). When Christ was born, God sent an angel to announce that salvation, saying, "Behold, I bring you good tidings of great joy, which shall be to all people. For unto you is born this day in the city of David a Saviour, which is Christ the Lord" (Luke 2: 10). There is only one way by which man can return to God. "Jesus saith unto him, I am the way, the truth, and the life: no man cometh unto the Father, but by Me" (John 14: 6). "All things are delivered to Me of My Father: and no man knoweth who the Son is, but the Father; and who the Father is, but the Son, and he to whom the Son will reveal Him" (Luke 10: 22). "For after that in the wisdom of God the world by wisdom knew not God, it pleased God by the foolishness of preaching to save them that believe" (1 Cor. 1: 21). In his epistle to the Corinthians, Paul says, "And I, brethren, when I came to you, came not with excellency of speech, or of wisdom, declaring unto you the testimony of God. For I determined not to know any thing among you, save Jesus Christ, and Him crucified" (1 Cor. 2: 1). To the Romans Paul writes, " I am not ashamed of the Gospel of Christ, for it is the power of God unto salvation to every one that believeth" (Rom. 1: 16). "So then, faith cometh by hearing, and hearing by the Word of God" (Rom. 1: 17).

Christ sends His disciples to deliver a certain message in His name. When the Lord sent Jonah to Nineveh, he said unto him, "Arise, go unto Nineveh, that great city, and preach unto it the preaching that I bid thee." Jonah did not, as is too much the case nowadays, offer bribes or inducements to the people of Nineveh to come and hear him. But Jonah arose, and went unto Nineveh, according to the word of the Lord. Now, Nineveh was an exceeding great city of three days' journey. And Jonah began to enter into the city a day's journey, and he cried and said, "Yet forty days, and Nineveh shall be overthrown" (Jonah 3: 1). The result was, the people believed God, proclaimed a fast, put on sack-cloth, and turned from their evil way and were forgiven. On the day of Pentecost, when the Apostles began to preach in Jerusalem, no bribes or inducements were offered to draw men to hear the Gospel. According to the command of Jesus, they remained in prayer with the disciples, until they received power from the Holy Ghost. When they recived that power they commenced preaching Christ, using almost entirely words from that portion of the Holy Scriptures known to us as the Old Testament, foretelling the coming of Christ, and the outpouring of the Holy Spirit. Telling them that Christ had come; and they, although they had seen the signs and wonders attesting Him, had rejected Him. "Him being delivered by the determinate counsel and foreknowledge of God ye have taken and by wicked hands have crucified and slain." "This Jesus hath God raised up, whereof we all are witnesses. Therefore being by the right hand of God exalted, and having received of the Father the promise of the Holy Ghost, He hath shed forth this, which ye now see and hear." * * "Therefore, let all the house of Israel know, assuredly, that God hath made that same Jesus, whom ye have crucified, both Lord and Christ. Now, when they heard this, they were pricked in their heart, and said unto Peter and to the rest of the apostles, Men and brethren what shall we do? Then Peter said unto them, Repent, and be baptized every one of you in the name of Jesus Christ for the remission of sins, and ye shall receive the gift of the Holy Ghost. * * * And the same day there were added unto them about three thousand souls" (Acts 2: 14-41). Immediately after the day of Pentecost, Peter preached again, using almost the same words; and the record says, "Many of them which heard the word believed, and the number of men was about five thousand" (Acts 3: 12-26; 4: 4). Since that time, in all countries, and in all ages, where the same Gospel has been faithfully preached, the same results have followed. Luther in Germany, John Knox in Scotland, John Wesley in England, Whitfield and Moody, by preaching Christ and the simple Gospel, have been the means of bringing tens of thousands to Christ. The great aim of these reformers was not to reform men, but to renew them; not to attack specific sins, but to destroy the root of every sin by a change of the heart. This they accomplished by preaching Christ, and the doctrines of grace; the only way to reform and to elevate man. The only way ordained by Christ to save man. The only way attended and made effectual by the power of the Holy Ghost.

These results have always followed preaching Christ among the heathen. The Moravians labored in Greenland for several years without success. One of them, while translating Matthew's Gospel, was visited by a number of the natives, who desired to know the contents of the book. The missionary gratified their desire; told them of man's fall by sin, and his recovery by Christ; enlarged with energy and feeling upon the price of redemption, and then read from the book in his hand the history of our Saviour's agony in the garden. The account goes on to state, "Now, the Spirit of God began to work," and from that time the work went on with great speed and power, and a large number of consistent and steadfast converts were made. The same results followed the preaching of David Brainerd, who died over a century ago, at the early age of twenty-nine; greatly beloved, and greatly lamented. His missionary labors were among the Indians in New Jersey. They were ignorant and stupid, steeped in sensuality, given over to the love of strong drink, without natural affection, and full of prejudices against white men. Their language was not known by the missionary, who was compelled to preach to them by an indifferent interpreter; and his instructions, when understood, were zealously opposed by wicked white men. Yet, notwithstanding all these obstacles, the Spirit of God was poured out upon them. Within the short space of eleven months, seventy-seven of these poor creatures were converted. From being drunken, howling savages, they became devout and intelligent Christians. Mr. Brainerd states in his remarks concerning the work:

"I can not but take notice that I have in

general, ever since my first coming among the Indians in New Jersey, been favored with that assistance which, to me, is *uncommon*, in preaching *Christ crucified*, and making Him the *centre* and *mark* to which all my discourses among them were directed.

"It was the principal scope and drift of all my discourses to this people for several months together, (after having taught them something of the *being* and *perfections* of God, His creation of man in a state of rectitude and happiness, and the obligations mankind were thence under to love and honor Him), to lead them into an acquaintance with their deplorable state by nature, *as fallen creatures ;* their *inability* to extricate and deliver themselves from it; the *utter insufficiency* of any *external* reformations and amendments of life, or of any religious performances of which *they* were capable, while in this state, to bring them into the favor of God, and interest them in His eternal mercy; thence to show them their *absolute* need of Christ, to redeem and save them from the misery of their fallen state; to open His *all-sufficiency* and willingness to save the chief of sinners; the *freeness* and *riches* of divine grace, proposed " without money and without price," to all who will accept the offer; thereupon to press them, *without delay*, to betake themselves to Him, under a sense of their misery and *undone* state, for relief and everlasting salvation; and to show them the abundant encouragement the Gospel proposes to needy, perishing, and helpless sinners, in order to *engage* them so to do. These things I repeatedly and largely insisted upon, from time to time.

"When these truths were felt *at heart*, there was now no vice unreformed, no external duty neglected. Drunkenness, the darling vice, was broken off from, and scarce an instance of it known among my hearers, for months together. The abusive practice of *husbands* and *wives*, in putting away each other, and taking others in their stead, was quickly reformed, so that there are three or four couple who have voluntarily dismissed those whom they had wrongfully taken, and now live together in love and peace. The same might be said of all other vicious practices. The reformation was general, and all springing from the *internal* influence of divine truths upon their hearts, and not from any *external* restraints, or because they had heard these vices particularly exposed and repeatedly spoken against. Some of them I never so much as mentioned, particularly that of the parting of men and their wives, till some, having their conscience awakened by God's word, came, and *of their own accord* confessed themselves guilty in that respect."—*Brainerd's Remarks, by Rev. Talbot W. Chambers.*

Wherever the Word of God is faithfully preached, God's law will be presented, and Christ offered, as the only way of salvation. The Lord Jesus has promised to be with him who delivers His message. The Holy Spirit will give power to the truth; then men will be convicted of sin, will be led to receive Christ, and will be saved. This is God's plan to save men. "And in none other is there salvation; for neither is there any other name under heaven, that is given among men, wherein we must be saved" (Acts 3: 12).

"As Moses lifted up the serpent in the wilderness, even so must the Son of man be lifted up; that whosoever believeth in Him may have eternal life" (John 3: 14). Men are perishing, and will die forever unless they look to Christ and believe in Him. "He that believeth not hath been judged already" (John 3: 18). "He that believeth on the Son hath everlasting life: and he that believeth not the Son shall not see life, but the wrath of God abideth on him" (John 3: 36).

SPECIAL CALLS OF GOD.

WHILE God "now commandeth all men everywhere to repent" (Acts 17: 30); in all ages He has made special calls on some. To all men, "The wrath of God is revealed from heaven against all ungodliness and unrighteousness of men, who hold the truth in unrighteousness. Because that which may be known of God is manifest in them; for God hath shewed it unto them. For the invisible things of Him from the creation of the world are clearly seen, being understood by the things that are made, even His eternal power and Godhead; so that they are without excuse" (Rom. 1: 18). "God, who at sundry times and in divers manners, spoke in time past unto the fathers by the prophets, hath in these last days spoken unto us by His Son, whom he hath appointed heir of all things, by whom also He made the worlds; who, being the brightness of His glory, and the express image of His person, and upholding all things by the word of his power, when He had by Himself purged our sins, sat down on the right hand of the majesty on high" (Heb. 1: 1). The great call of God to men is, to hear Him. "Lo! a voice from heaven saying, This is My beloved Son" (Matt. 3: 17). "This is My beloved Son, * * * hear ye Him" (Matt. 17: 5).

The Bible mentions many special calls of God to individuals. When Adam tried to hide himself, "The Lord God called unto Adam, and said unto him, Where art thou?" (Gen. 3: 9). "And the Lord said unto Noah, Come, thou, and all thy house into the ark" (Gen. 7: 1). "The Lord had said unto Abram, Get thee out of thy country, and from thy kindred, and from thy father's house, unto a land that I will shew thee" (Gen. 12: 1; 22: 15–22). "I called him alone and blessed him and prospered him" (Isai. 51: 2). "The angel of God called to Hagar out of heaven" (Gen. 21: 17). God called unto Moses out of the midst of the bush, and said, Moses, Moses" (Exod. 3: 4). "The Lord came, and stood, and called as at other times, Samuel, Samuel" (1 Sam. 3: 4, 6, 8, 10). Jesus called Paul, "And he heard a voice from heaven saying unto him, Saul, Saul, why persecutest thou Me? And he said, Who art Thou, Lord? And the Lord said, I am Jesus whom thou persecutest" (Acts 9: 4).

The Bible contains calls to all men. The call by Isaiah 750 years before Christ was, "Ho, every one that thirsteth, come ye to the waters, and he that hath no money; come ye, buy and eat; yea, come buy wine and milk without money and without price. Wherefore do ye spend money for that which is not bread? and your labour for that which satisfieth not? hearken diligently unto Me, and eat that which is good, and let your soul delight itself in fatness. Incline your ear, and come unto me; hear, and your soul shall live" (Isaiah 55: 1). The call by the Lord Jesus Christ is, "Come unto me, all ye that labor and are heavy laden, and I will give you rest. Take my yoke upon you, and learn of me; for I am meek and lowly in heart: and ye shall find rest unto your souls. For my yoke is easy, and my burden is light" (Matt. 11: 28). He also says, "Him that cometh to Me I will in nowise cast out" (John 6: 37). The call in the last chapter of the Bible is, "And the Spirit and the bride say, Come. And let him that heareth say, Come. And let him that is athirst come. And whosoever will, let him take the water of life freely" (Rev. 22: 17). Jesus "calleth His own sheep by name, and leadeth them out * * * He goeth before them, and the sheep follow Him: for they know His voice" (John 10: 4). "And we know that to them that love God all things work together for good, to them that are called according to His purpose. For whom He foreknew, He also foreordained to be conformed to the image of His Son, that he might be the firstborn among many brethren: and whom He foreordained, them He also called: and whom He called, them He also justified: and whom He justified, them He also glorified" (Rom. 8: 28). And Jesus " calleth unto him whom He would: and they came unto Him. And He ordained twelve, that they should be with Him, and that He might send them forth to preach " (Mark 3: 13). "Ye have not chosen me, but I have chosen you" (John 15: 16, 19; 6: 70; 13: 18). "The Master is come, and calleth for thee" (Luke 11: 28). "Faithful is He that calleth you, who also will do it" (1 Thess. 5: 24). "Who hath saved us, and called us with an holy calling, not according to our works, but according to His own purpose and grace, which was given us in Christ Jesus before the world began" (2 Tim. 1: 9).

God's calls to His people to give up their idolatry and return to Him, repeated again and again, in almost every age, are very touching, and full of pathos. They offer, like the Parable of the Prodigal Son, not only forgiveness, but a loving reception to the backslider and the fallen, if they will repent and turn to God. "My people are bent to backsliding from me. * * * How shall I give thee up, Ephraim? how shall I deliver thee, Israel? how shall I make thee as Admah? how shall I set thee as Zeboim? Mine heart is turned within me, my repentings are kindled together. I will not execute the fierceness of mine anger, I will not return to destroy Ephraim: for I am God, and not man" (Hosea 11: 7). "Is Ephraim my dear son? is he a pleasant child? for since I spake against him, I do earnestly remember him still; therefore my bowels are troubled for him: I will surely have mercy upon him, saith the LORD" (Jer. 31: 20). "O Israel, thou shalt not be forgotten of me. I have blotted out, as a thick cloud, thy transgressions, and, as a cloud, thy sins: return unto me; for I have redeemed thee" (Isai. 44: 21). "Return, thou backsliding Israel, saith the LORD, and I will not cause mine anger to fall upon you: for I am merciful, saith the LORD" (Jer. 3: 12). "Return, ye backsliding children, and I will heal your backsliding" (Jer. 3: 22). "I have spoken unto you, rising early, and speaking; but ye hearkened not unto me. I have sent also unto you all my servants the prophets, rising up early and sending them, saying, Return ye now every man from his evil way, and amend your doings, and go not after other gods to serve them" (Jer. 35: 14). "For why will ye die, O house of Israel? For I have no pleasure in the death of him that dieth, saith the Lord God: wherefore turn yourselves, and live ye" (Ezek. 18: 31). "Now, therefore, if ye will obey my voice indeed, and keep my covenant, then ye shall be a peculiar treasure unto me above all people: for all the earth is mine. And ye shall be unto me a kingdom of priests, and an holy nation" (Exod. 19: 5). "For thou art an holy people unto the LORD, thy God, and the LORD hath chosen thee to be a peculiar people unto Himself, above all the nations that are upon the earth" (Deut. 14: 2). "But ye are are a chosen generation, a royal priesthood, an holy nation, a peculiar people: that ye should show forth the praises of Him who hath called you out of darkness into His marvellous light" (1 Pet. 2: 9).

"Wherefore come out from among them, and be ye separate, saith the Lord, touch not the unclean thing; and I will receive you, and will be a Father unto you, and ye shall be my sons and daughters, saith the Lord Almighty" (2 Cor. 6: 17). "And the God of all grace, who hath called you unto His eternal glory in Christ, after that ye have suffered awhile, shall Himself perfect, stablish, strengthen you. To Him be the dominion for ever and ever. Amen" (1 Pet. 5: 10).

GOD COMMANDETH ALL MEN EVERYWHERE TO REPENT.

Man, a sinner by nature and by practice, "is condemned already" (John 3: 18). And "the wrath of God abideth on him" (John 3: 36). While he remains in rebellion against God, he is increasing his guilt and his indebtedness every moment of his existence. He takes advantage of the long suffering of God "to usward, not willing that any should perish, but that all should come to repentance" (2 Pet. 3: 9). Proving, as the Word of God says, that "Because sentence against an evil work is not executed speedily, therefore the heart of the sons of men is fully set in them to do evil" (Eccl. 8: 11). God "now commandeth all men everywhere to repent: because He hath appointed a day; in the which He will judge the world" (Acts 17: 30).

The first step to save men is to convict them of sin. Unless this is done, they will not repent and will not accept Christ. The first work of the Holy Spirit is, "He will convict the world of sin" (John 16: 8). The first preaching to men recorded in the New Testament was commanding them to repent. No baits were offered to allure men to come and hear the Gospel, as is being done at the present time. The messenger was sent by God, to deliver the message of God. Repent! for you are lost. It is to be remembered that these messengers and the messages were sent first to the church. "And that repentance and remission of sins should be preached in His name among all nations, beginning at Jerusalem" (Luke 24: 47). John the Baptist began preaching, saying, "Repent ye: for the kingdom of heaven is at hand" (Matt. 3: 1). And "Jesus came into Galilee, preaching the gospel of the kingdom of God, and saying, the time is fulfilled, and the kingdom of God is at hand: repent ye, and believe the Gospel" (Mark 1: 14). "And He called unto Him the twelve, and began to send them forth two and two." "And they went out and preached that men should repent" (Mark 6: 7, 12). On the day of Pentecost, after Peter's preaching, the record says, "Now when they heard this, they were pricked in their heart, and said unto Peter and to the rest of the apostles, Men and brethren, what shall we do? Then Peter said unto them, Repent, and be baptized every one of you in the name of Jesus Christ for the remission of sins, and ye shall receive the gift of the Holy Ghost" (Acts 2: 37). And again he says, "Repent ye therefore, and be converted, that your sins may be blotted out, when the times of refreshing shall come from the presence of the Lord; and He shall send Jesus Christ which before was preached unto you" (Acts 3: 19). Paul says, God "now commandeth all men everywhere to repent:

because He hath appointed a day, in the which He will judge the world in righteousness by that man whom He hath ordained; whereof He hath given assurance unto all men, in that He hath raised Him from the dead" (Acts 17: 30). Jesus said unto Paul, "I have appeared unto thee for this purpose, to make thee a minister and a witness both of these things which thou hast seen, and of those things in the which I will appear unto thee; delivering thee from the people, and from the gentiles, unto whom now I send thee, to open their eyes, and to turn them from darkness to light, and from the power of Satan unto God, that they may receive forgiveness of sins, and inheritance among them which are sanctified by faith that is in me" (Acts 26: 16). Paul, speaking of this vision to Agrippa, adds, "Whereupon, O King Agrippa, I was not disobedient unto the heavenly vision, but shewed first unto them of Damascus, and at Jerusalem, and throughout all the coasts of Judea, and then to the Gentiles, that they should repent and turn to God, and do works meet for repentance" (Acts 26: 19).

The first duty of every messenger of God to men is to call them to repentance. This same message is to be delivered in the palaces or the slums; in the churches and in the highways. This must be first. The giving of food, washing and clothing the poor, and giving them ethical culture, may follow, as the fruits of the Gospel, but must not be put before it. "Say unto them, As I live, saith the Lord God, I have no pleasure in the death of the wicked; but that the wicked turn from his way and live: turn ye, turn ye from your evil ways; for why will ye die, O house of Israel?" (Ezek. 33: 11).

Baptism, confirmation, taking the communion, joining the church, do not regenerate, or make children of God. They who depend on these things, as was the case with the rulers and teachers in the church in the days of Christ, not only cannot enter into the kingdom of God, but do not see it; do not know what the kingdom of God is. Talking with Nicodemus, a ruler in the church, "Jesus answered and said unto him, Verily, verily, I say unto thee, except a man be born anew (from above), he cannot see the kingdom of God" (John 3: 3). In all ages the great danger has been, having false teachers and rulers in the church, deceiving the people by putting their traditions in the place of the Scriptures and leading their followers into idolatry. Jeremiah writes of the church in his day, "From the least even unto the greatest of them every one is given to covetousness; and from the prophet even unto the priest every one dealeth falsely. They have healed also the hurt of the daughter of my people slightly, saying, Peace, peace; when there is no peace" (Jer. 6: 13). John the Baptist said to the leaders of the church in his day, who had come to his baptism, "O generation of vipers, who hath warned you to flee from the wrath to come?" (Matt. 3: 7; Mark 3: 7, 8).

In the twenty-third chapter of Matthew we have an account of the rulers of the church in the days when Christ was on the earth. Jesus warns the people against them and their teachings. He charges these rulers with "binding heavy burdens and grievous to be borne on men's shoulders;" "doing all their work to be seen of men," "making broad their phylacteries and enlarging the borders of their garments;" "loving the uppermost rooms of feasts and the chief seats in the Synagogue, and greetings in the market, and to be called of men, Rabbi, Rabbi." He tells the people, "call no man father upon the earth: for one is your Father which is is heaven." He then denounces the most fearful woes against those rulers and teachers. "Woe unto you, Scribes and Pharisees, hypocrites! for ye shut up the Kingdom of Heaven against men: for ye neither go in yourselves, neither suffer ye them that are entering to go in. Woe unto you, Scribes and Pharisees, hypocrites! for ye devour widows houses, and for a pretence make long prayer; therefore ye shall receive the greater damnation. Woe unto you, Scribes and Pharisees, hypocrites! for ye compass sea and land to make one proselyte; and when he is made, ye make him two-fold more the child of hell than yourselves." "Ye serpents, ye generation of vipers, how can ye escape the damnation of hell" (Matt. 23)?

The descriptions of the church in the days of Jeremiah, John the Baptist and Christ, applicable to the largest portion of the church at the present time. What is needed is another John the Baptist to call the churches to repentance, and "to make ready a people prepared for the Lord" (Luke 1: 16, 17).

The Bible teaches us that being born in a church, or being baptized, or being zealous and a strict observer of all the rules of the church, or even being as Cornelius was, "A devout man, and one that feared God with all his house, which gave much alms to the people, and prayed always" (Acts 10: 27) are none, or all of them, sufficient to save men. We are told a certain man called Simon, believed and was baptized. Yet he was afterwards told by Peter, "I perceive that thou art in the gall of bitterness, and in the bond of iniquity" (Acts 8: 9, 13, 23). Being zealous in church services or ordinances, and reading the Scriptures cannot save men. The Ethiopian eunuch had gone to Jerusalem to worship; and while returning, was reading Isaiah. It was necessary to send an angel to Philip, directing him to go and explain the Scripture to him. Philip did so, and began at the same Scripture and preached unto him Jesus. The eunuch believed, was baptized, and went on his way rejoicing (Acts 8: 26). In his case, his going to Jerusalem and worshipping there, was not enough; his studying the Scriptures was not enough; his belief in his church was not enough; a special miracle must be done to make him know Christ; that he might be saved. The case of Cornelius, a centurion of the band called the Italian band, shows, that being devout, fearing God, giving alms and praying to God always, is not enough to save a man, without the knowledge of Christ, and believing Him. It required two miracles to save him. An angel of God came to him and told him to send for Peter and he would tell him what to do. Special visions appeared to Peter, and the voice of the Spirit directed him to go with the messengers sent by Cornelius. He went, and preached Christ unto him; and the Holy Ghost fell on all them which heard the word; and they were baptized. Peter in relating the occurence, adds, "The angel told Cornelius that Peter shall tell thee words whereby thou and all thy house shall be saved" (Acts 11: 14). This teaches us that, being devout, and one that feared God with all his house, and giving much alms, and praying to God always, is not sufficient for salvation. It was necessary to hear the Gospel, to be saved. His prayers were heard, and God sent Peter to preach Christ to him; and the Holy Ghost was given, and he was saved. Living a moral life cannot save a man. One came running and kneeled to Christ asking, what shall I do to inherit eternal life? Jesus referred him to the commandments; quoting the last six speaking of our duty towards men. He answered, "All these have I observed from my youth." Then "Jesus beholding him, loved him, and said unto him, One thing thou lackest." He told him to do certain things, closing with, "And come, take up thy cross, and follow me. And he was sad at that saying, and went away grieved; for he had great possessions" (Mark 10: 17). Being circumcised, or baptized, and being zealous in observing all the forms, ceremonies, &c., of the church does not make a person a child of God; and cannot save anyone. Paul says, "If any other man thinketh that he hath whereof he might trust in the flesh, I more: circumcised the eighth day, of the stock of Israel, of the tribe of Benjamin, a Hebrew of the Hebrews; as touching the law, a Pharisee; concerning zeal, persecuting the church; touching the righteousness which is in the law, blameless. But what things were gain to me, those I counted loss for Christ. Yea doubtless, and I count all things but loss for the excellency of the knowledge of Christ Jesus, my Lord: for whom I have suffered the loss of all things, and do count them but dung, that I may win Christ, and be found in Him, not having my own righteousness, which is of the law, but that which is through the faith of Christ, the righteousness which is of God by faith" (Phil. 3: 4). Vast multitudes of members of the church think that they are children of God, and are resting their hope of salvation on those things, which Paul, when converted, counted "as dung." A special appearance of the Lord Jesus Christ to Paul caused his conversion, and was the means of his being saved.

All the above cases were men conspicuous in the church, and of high standing in it; yet miracles were necessary to bring them to Christ. The command to all men, in the church and out of it, is, repent and believe in the Lord Jesus Christ. The greatest need at the present time is repentance in the churches. Then the command to repent will be carried to the lapsed masses. And then we may look for the miracle of men being born again of the Holy Ghost.

CHILDREN OF GOD BORN AGAIN.

Man is born with a corrupt nature, alienated from God: and although God has provided redemption for him, and "beseeches" him to accept that redemption and "be reconciled to God" (II Cor. 5. 20), he will not do so, unless the Holy Spirit changes his heart. The reason is, "The carnal mind is enmity against God" (Rom. 8: 7). Men are "haters of God" (Rom. 1: 30). Christ told His disciples, "If the world hate you, ye know that it hated Me before it hated you" "He that hateth Me, hateth my Father also." " Now have they both seen and hated both Me and my Father" (John 15: 18, 23, 24). Therefore the Bible tells us, that men to be saved, need not only the Gospel call, "Repent and believe in the Lord Jesus Christ;" but that the call will be in vain, and men will not believe, unless the word is made effectual by the Holy Spirit. "For by grace are ye saved through faith; and that not of yourselves: it is the gift of God" (Eph. 2: 8).

According to the Scriptures, a man to be saved, must be "Born again;" "Created anew;" "Raised from the dead." Christ told Nicodemus, a ruler of the Jews, "Verily, verily, I say unto thee, except a man be born again, he cannot see the kingdom of God." "Except a man be born of water and of the Spirit, he cannot enter into the kingdom of God" (John 3: 3, 5). John speaking of Jesus says, "He was in the world, and the world was made by Him, and the world knew Him not. He came unto His own, and His own received Him not. But as many as received Him, to them gave He the right to become Children of God, even to them that believe on His name which were born, not of blood, nor of the will of the flesh, nor of the will of man, but of God" (John 1: 11). That is, not by natural descent or birth; nor by their own will; not by the will of any priest by baptism, or confirmation; or the will of any man; but of God. "To as many as received Him." To receive Christ, we must know Him as He is revealed in the Scriptures; we must know Him as did Peter when he said, " Thou art the Christ, the Son of the living God." When we know this, Jesus says to us, as He did to Peter, "Blessed art thou, Simon Barjona; for flesh and blood hath not revealed it unto thee, but my Father which is in heaven" (Matt. 16: 16). No one receives Him, who does not believe in His name, The Lord Jesus Christ. Isaiah, 700 years before Christ, announced His Name. "Behold a virgin shall conceive and bear a son, and shall call his name Immanuel" (Isa. 7: 14), "which is being interpreted, God with us" (Matt. 1: 23). "And she shall bring forth a son; and thou shalt call His name Jesus; for it is He that shall save His people from their sins" (Matt. 1: 21). "For unto us a child is born, unto us a son is given; and the government shall be upon his shoulder; and his name shall be called Wonderful, Counsellor, The Mighty God, The Everlasting Father, (Father of Eternity), The Prince of Peace" (Isa. 9: 6). If we have recieved Him and believe on His Name, He has given us the right to become children of God (John 1: 12).

They who regard Him only as a good man, or as an example, do not receive Him; they deny Him. He must be known and received as He is revealed and offered in the Word of God, or He is not received at all. Peter explains how we become children of God. "Being born again not of corruptible seed, but of incorruptible, by the Word of God" (I Peter 1: 23). Jesus says, "That which is born of the flesh is flesh; and that which is born of the Spirit is Spirit" (John 3: 6). John says, "Whosoever believeth that Jesus is the Christ is born of God" (I John 5: 1; Gal 3: 26). Paul says, "As many as are led by the Spirit of God, they are the Sons of God." "The Spirit itself beareth witness with our Spirit, that we are the children of God" (Rom. 8: 14, 16). "Blessed be the God and Father of our Lord Jesus Christ, which according to his abundant mercy hath begotten us again into a lively hope by the resurrection of Jesus Christ from the dead, to an inheritance incorruptible, and nndefiled, and that fadeth not away, reserved in heaven for you, who are kept by the power of God through faith unto salvation ready to be revealed in the last time" (I Peter 1: 3). "Beloved, now are we the Sons of God, and it doth not yet appear what we shall be; but we know that, when He shall appear, we shall be like Him; for we shall see Him as He is. And every man that hath this hope in him, purifieth himself, even as He is pure" (I John 3: 2).

CHILDREN OF GOD CREATED ANEW.

The Scriptures also tell us, that the children of God are created anew. David prayed, "Create in one a clean heart, O God" (Ps 51: 10). God says, "I will put a new Spirit within you; and I will take the stony heart out of their flesh, and will give them a heart of flesh" (Ezek. 11: 19). "A new heart also will I give you, and a new Spirit will I put within you; and I will take away the stony heart out of your flesh, and I will give you a heart of flesh" (Ezek. 36: 26). It is written, "If any man be in Christ, he is a new creature; old things are passed away; behold all things are become new, and all things are of God, who hath reconciled us to Himself by Jesus Christ" (II Cor. 5: 17). "For in Christ Jesus neither circumcision, availeth anything, nor uncircumcision, but a new creature" (Gal. 6: 15). "For by grace are ye saved through faith: and that not of yourselves: it is the gift of God: not of works, lest any man should boast. For we are His workmanship, created in Christ Jesus unto good works, which God hath before ordained that we should walk in them" (Eph. 2: 6-10). Reader, have you been born anew? Created anew? Have you been "renewed in the Spirit of your mind?" Have you "put on the new man which after God is created in righteousness and true holiness" (Eph. 4: 24)? "The new man, which is renewed in knowledge after the image of Him that created him" (Col. 3: 10).

CHILDREN OF GOD MADE ALIVE FROM THE DEAD.

The Scriptures tell us that the children of God are born again, are created anew, and also, made alive from the dead. No stronger language can be used to show that the work of redemption is entirely, from beginning to end, of God. No child has ever caused its own birth; no creature has created itself; no dead thing has ever brought itself to life. In Ezekiel we have a vivid description of the state of the natural man, and of the church at times. He saw a valley full of bones and they were very dry. And He was commanded to say unto them, "O ye dry bones, hear the word of the Lord. Thus saith the Lord God unto these bones, "behold I will cause breath to enter into you, and ye shall live." * * * "And ye shall know that I am the Lord." He prophesied accordingly, and, "behold a shaking, and the bones came together, bone to his bone." * * * "The sinews and the flesh came up upon them, and the skin covered them above; but there was no breath in them." He was commanded to prophecy again, and he did so, "and the breath came into them and they lived." (Ezek. 37: 1-14). "Wherefore he saith, awake thou that sleepest, and arise from the dead, and

Christ shall give thee light." (Eph. 5: 14). Jesus says, "Verily, verily, I say unto you, he that heareth my Word, and believeth on Him that sent me, hath everlasting life, and shall not come into condemnation; but is passed from death unto life" (John 5: 24). "He that believeth not the Son shall not see life; but the wrath of God abideth on him" (John 3: 36). Believers in Christ Jesus are told, "You hath he quickened, who were dead in trespasses and sins; wherein in time past ye walked according to the course of this world, according to the prince of the power of the air, the spirit that now worketh in the children of disobedience: among whom also we all had our conversation in times past in the lusts of our flesh, fulfilling the desires of the flesh and of the mind; and were by nature children of wrath, even as others. But God, who is rich in mercy, for his great love wherewith He loved us, even when we were dead in sins, hath quickened us together with Christ (by grace ye are saved); and hath raised us up together, and made us sit together in Heavenly places in Christ Jesus" (Eph. 2: 1).

THE CHILDREN OF GOD CHOSEN BY HIM BEFORE THE FOUNDATION OF THE WORLD.

WE have seen that the children of God, are born again; created anew; raised from the dead; and that this is not by their own will, nor by the will of others, but of God. The children of God are chosen in Christ before the foundation of the world; not because they were holy; or because of good works, "lest they should boast," but they "were created in Christ Jesus unto good works," and that they "should be holy." Paul writes, to the saints which are at Ephesus and to the faithful in Christ Jesus, "Blessed be the God and Father of our Lord Jesus Christ, who hath blessed us with all spiritual blessings in Heavenly places in Christ: according as he hath chosen us in him, before the foundation of the world, that we should be holy and without blame before Him in love; having predestinated us unto the adoption of children by Jesus Christ to himself, according to the good pleasure of his will, to the praise of the glory of His grace, wherein he hath made us accepted in the beloved: in whom we have redemption through his blood, the forgiveness of sins, according to the riches of his grace" (Eph. 1: 1-12). Paul then tells them, of the "exceeding greatness of his power to us-ward who believe, according to the working of his mighty power which he wrought in Christ when he raised him from the dead and set him at his own right hand in the heavenly places, far above all principality, and power, and might and dominion, and every name that is named, not only in this world, but also in that which is to come: and hath put all things under his feet, and gave him to be the head over all things to the church, which is his body, the fulness of him that filleth all in all. And you hath he quickened who were dead in trespasses and sins. * * * But God who is rich in mercy, for his great love wherewith he loved us, even when we were dead in sins, hath quickened us together with Christ. * * * For by grace are ye saved through faith; and that not of yourselves; it is the gift of God: not of works, lest any man should boast. For we are his workmanship, created in Christ Jesus unto good works, which God hath before ordained that we should walk in them" (Eph. 1: 19; 2: 1, 4, 8). To the "beloved of God, called saints," in Rome, the same truth is taught. "We know that all things work together for good to them that love God, to them who are the called according to his purpose. For whom he did foreknow, he also did predestinate to be conformed to the image of his son, that he might be the firstborn among many brethren. Moreover, whom he did predestinate, them he also called: and whom he called, them he also justified: and whom he justified, them he also glorified" (Rom. 8: 28). We are told that, "Faith cometh by hearing, and hearing by the word of God" (Rom. 10: 17). "To the Church of God, which is at Corinth," Paul writes, "Christ sent me not to baptize, but to preach the gespel; not with wisdom of words, lest the cross of Christ should be made of none effect. For the preaching of the cross is to them that perish, foolishness; but unto us which are saved, it is the power of God. For it is written, I will destroy the wisdom of the wise, and will bring to nothing the understanding of the prudent. Where is the wise? Where is the Scribe? Where is the disputer of this world? Hath not God made foolish the wisdom of this world? For after that in the wisdom of God the world by wisdom knew not God, it pleased God by the foolishness of preaching to save them that believe" (I Cor. 1: 17). To the church in Rome Paul writes, "So, as much as in me is, I am ready to preach the Gospel to you that are at Rome also. For I am not ashamed of the gospel of Christ: for it is the power of God unto salvation to every one that believeth; to the Jew first, and also to the Greek. For therein is the righteousness of God revealed from faith to faith: as it is written, The just shall live by faith" (Rom. 1: 15). God at creation made all things by His word. He spake and it was done. He said,

"Let there be light, and there was light" (Gen. 1: 3). Ever since the word of God gives life and light to men, "the entrance of Thy word giveth light" (Ps. 119: 130). "God, who commanded the light to shine out of darkness, hath shined in our hearts, to give the light of the knowledge of the glory of God in the face of Jesus Christ" (2 Cor. 4: 6). "For ye were sometimes darkness, but now are ye light in the Lord" (Eph. 5: 8). The word of God from the beginning was Christ. "The word was made flesh and dwelt among us" (John 1: 1-14). He is the Word of God to give life and light to men. And therefore Paul preached Christ; and Christians are to be witnesses for Christ; Timothy was charged, "Preach the Word; be instant in season, out of season; reprove, rebuke, exhort with all long suffering and doctrine" (2 Tim. 4: 2). Child of God! born again, made alive, created anew, by the Word of God; that word is committed to you; that you may grow thereby, and by means of it save others. Use that word; for God says, comparing it to the rain that watereth the earth, and maketh it bring forth and bud, that it may give seed to the sower, and bread to the eater, "So shall my word be that goeth forth out of my mouth: it shall not return unto me void, but it shall accomplish that which I please, and it shall prosper in thing whereto I sent it" (Isa. 55: 11).

FAITH AND GOOD WORKS.

God's way of salvation differs from that of every other religion in the world, including those of the lapsed churches. God's plan is Salvation by faith. All other religions look to their good works for salvation. The children of God are told to do good works not in order to be saved, but because they are saved. Cain's offering of his own productions was rejected by God. Abel's offering which we are told was by faith, was accepted. Sacrifices for sin were required by God as a part of every act of worship. For sins of commission, of omission, of ignorance, of presumption; sin-offerings daily, on the Sabbath Day, and even when presenting thank offerings and national thanksgivings. All these sacrifices represented the Lord Jesus Christ, "the lamb slain from the foundation of the world" (Rev. 13: 8). The Lamb of God, which taketh away the sin of the world" (John 1: 29). "Christ our passover is sacrificed for us" (1 Cor. 5: 8). The Lamb now on the throne, as described in Revelations, as "a Lamb standing, as though it had been slain" (Rev. 5: 6). In the eleventh chapter of the Epistle to the Hebrews we have a list of the patriarchs and worthies in the Old Testament, commended for their faith. In all these cases their good works are spoken of as the result of their faith. Elsewhere we are told, "If Abraham were justified by works, he hath whereof to glory; but not before God. For what saith the Scripture? Abraham believed God, and it was counted unto him for righteousness" (Rom. 4: 2). "Without faith it is impossible to please God" (Heb. 11: 6). The same motive for doing good works is in the Old Testament as in the New. In the Old, God continually reminds his people, that because he had delivered them from Egypt, they should love, and obey Him. The introduction of the Ten Commandments begins with, "I am the Lord thy God, which have brought thee out of the Land of Egypt, out of the house of bondage. Thou shalt have no other Gods before Me. Thou shalt not &c., &c." (Exod. 20: 2). The children of Israel are constantly reminded of this deliverance as an incentive to obedience and good works (Exod. 13: 3, 9, 14, 16; Deut. 6: 21; Levit. 19: 36; Num. 15: 40, 41; Ps. 81: 10; Deut. 5: 15; Josh. 24: 5 &c). They are also told that the Lord had redeemed them out of the house of bondage and led them forth and guided them in His strength unto His holy habitation (Exod. 15: 13; Deut. 7: 8; 15: 15; 9: 26; 24: 18; &c., &c). The same reasons, in almost the same words, are used in the New Testament calling upon the children of God to love Him, and do good works; not in order to save themselves, but because God through the Lord Jesus Christ has saved them.

"That no man is justified by the law in the sight of God, it is evident; for the just shall live by faith." "Christ hath redeemed us from the curse of the law, being made a curse for us." "That we might receive the promise of the Spirit through faith" (Gal. 3: 11, 13, 14). "Be ye holy; for I am holy." "Forasmuch as ye know that ye were not redeemed with corruptible things, as silver and gold, from your vain conversation received by tradition from your fathers; but with the precious blood of Christ, as of a lamb without blemish and without spot; who verily was foreordained before the foundation of the world" (1 Pet. 1: 16, 18). "Who hath delivered from the power of darkness, and hath translated us into the kingdom of His dear Son. In whom we have redemption through His blood even the forgiveness of sins" (Col. 1: 13). "Jesus which delivered us from the wrath to come" (1 Thess. 1: 10). "Ye are bought with a price: therefore glorify God in your body, and in your Spirit, which are God's" (1 Cor. 6: 20). "Thanks be to God, which giveth us the victory through our Lord Jesus Christ. Therefore, my beloved brethren, be ye steadfast, unmoveable, always abounding in the work of the Lord, forasmuch as ye know that your labour is not in vain in the Lord" (1 Cor. 15: 58). "Therefore, as ye abound in everything, in faith, and utterance, and knowledge, and in all diligence, and in your love to us, see that ye abound in this grace also." "For ye know the grace of our Lord Jesus Christ, that though He was rich, yet for your sakes He became poor, that ye through His poverty might be rich" (2 Cor. 8: 7, 9). We are told, "Work out your own salvation with fear and trembling; for it is God which worketh in you both to will and to do of His good pleasure;" work, not to be saved, but because ye have salvation, work it out. "Let no man deceive you with vain words: for because of these things cometh the wrath of God upon the children of disobedience. Be not therefore partakers with them. For ye were sometime darkness, but now are ye light in the Lord: walk as children of light" (Eph. 5: 6). "Reckon ye yourselves to be dead indeed unto sin, but alive unto God through Jesus Christ our Lord. Let not sin, therefore, reign in your mortal body, that ye should obey it in the lusts thereof" (Rom. 6: 12). "I beseech you therefore, brethren, by the mercies of God, that ye present your bodies, a living sacrifice, holy, acceptable unto God, which is your reasonable service" (Rom. 12: 1). "Having therefore these promises, dearly beloved, let us cleanse ourselves from all filthiness of the flesh and spirit, perfecting holiness in the fear of God" (2 Cor. 7: 1). "Now, therefore, ye are no more strangers and foreigners, but fellow citizens of the saints, and of the household of God; and are built upon the foundation of the apostles and prophets, Jesus Christ Himself being the chief cornerstone, in whom ye are builded together for an habitation of God through the Spirit. For this cause, I, Paul, the prisoner of Jesus Christ, for you Gentiles, beseech you that ye walk worthy of the vocation wherewith ye are called, with all lowliness and meekness, with long suffering, forbearing one another in love; endeavoring to keep the unity of the Spirit in the bond of peace." "Be ye therefore followers of God, as dear children." "Do all things without murmurings and disputings, that ye may be blameless and harmless, the songs of God, without rebuke, in midst of a crooked and perverse nation, among whom ye shine as lights in the world." "For our conversation is in heaven; from whence also we look for the Saviour, the Lord Jesus Christ: who shall change our vile body, that it may be fashioned like unto his glorious body, according to the working whereby he is able even to subdue all things unto himself. Therefore, my brethren, dearly beloved and longed for, my joy and crown, so stand fast in the Lord, dearly beloved."

"If ye then be risen with Christ, seek those things which are above, where Christ sitteth at the right hand of God. Set your affections on things above, not on things on the earth, for ye are dead, and your life is hid with Christ in God." "Put on therefore, as the elect of God, holy and beloved, bowels of mercies, kindness, humbleness of mind, meekness, long-suffering; forbearing one another, and forgiving one another, if any man have a quarrel against any: even as Christ forgave you, so also do ye. And above all things put on charity, which is the bond of perfectness." "Whatsoever ye do in word or deed, do all in the name of the Lord Jesus, giving thanks to God and the Father by him." "Ye are all the children of light, and the children of the day; we are not of the night nor of darkness. Therefore let us not sleep, as do others, but let us watch and be sober." "Ye are a chosen generation, a royal priesthood, an holy nation, a peculiar people, that ye should show forth the praises (virtues) of him who hath called you out of darkness into his marvelous light." " Nevertheless we, according to his promise, look for new heavens and a new earth, wherein dwelleth righteousness. Wherefore, beloved, seeing that ye look for such things, be diligent, that ye may be found of him in peace, without spot, and blameless." "Beloved now are we the sons of God; and it doth not yet appear what we shall be; but we know that when He shall appear, we shall be like him, for we shall see him as He is. And every man that hath this hope in him purifieth himself, even as He is pure."

Faith in Jesus Christ always works. "For in Jesus Christ neither circumcision availeth anything, nor uncircumcision ; but faith which worketh by love" (Gal. 5: 6). "Faith without works is dead" "Faith, if it hath not works is dead, being alone," ("in itself") (James 2: 17, 20).

Faith in Christ, "works by love," "purifies the heart" (Acts 15: 9; 1 John 3: 3); and "overcometh the world." "For whatsoever is born of God overcometh the world; and this is the victory that overcometh the world, even our faith. Who is he that overcometh the world, but he that believeth that Jesus is the Son of God" (1 John 5: 4)? "Without faith it is impossible to please God" (Heb. 11: 6). "For whatsoever is not of faith is sin" (Rom. 14: 23).

In working out the salvation which we have received from God, we must with filial fear and reverence, look to God continually, to work in us to will, and work in us the power to do, of His good pleasure. Salvation from beginning to end is of God.

"Enoch walked with God" (Gen. 5: 24). "By faith Enoch was translated that he should not see death; and he was not found, because God translated him; for before his translation he had this testimony that he pleased God" (Heb. 11: 5). Walking by faith with God, every believer may know that he pleases God. "The Lord taketh pleasure in his people" (Ps. 149: 4). "The Lord taketh pleasure in them that fear Him" (Ps. 147: 11). In his epistle to the Colossians Paul writes, "We do not cease to pray for you, and to desire that ye might be filled with the knowledge of his will in all wisdom and spiritual understanding; that ye might walk worthy of the Lord unto all pleasing, being fruitful in every good work, and increasing in the knowledge of God; strengthened with all might, according to his glorious power" (Col. 1: 9).

THE CHILDREN OF GOD HAVE ETERNAL LIFE NOW.

The children of Israel, when delivered from the bondage of Egypt, might have entered the promised land at once; but because of their unbelief, were compelled to wander in the wilderness forty years, and the most of them never entered it. "So we see that they could not enter in because of unbelief" (Heb. 3: 19). "Let us therefore fear, lest, a promise being left us of entering into his rest, any of you should seem to come short of it." "For we which have believed do enter into rest" (Heb. 4: 1, 3). Many children of God wander through the wilderness, troubled with doubts and fears, who, if they believed the promises connected with faith in the Lord Jesus Christ, would be enjoying a life of rest, joy, and peace. They do not realize that their salvation is sure the moment they believe; and is forever. That all the promises connected with faith, are in the present tense, and are to be enjoyed now, as well as hereafter. He that believeth HATH; he that believeth IS; and it is because they HAVE and because they ARE, that the Scriptures urge believers to glorify God, to rejoice in the Lord, and to do good works. Jesus said, "Verily, verily, I say unto you, He that heareth my word, and believeth on him that sent me, hath everlasting life, and shall not come into condemnation; but is passed from death unto life" (John 5: 24). "He that believeth on me hath everlasting life" (John 6: 47). "Being justified by faith, we have peace with God through our Lord Jesus Christ" (Rom. 5: 1). "He that believeth on the Son hath everlasting life" (John 3: 36). "Beloved, now are we the Sons of God, and it doth not yet appear what we shall be; but we know that, when he shall appear, we shall be like him; for we shall see him as he is. And every man that hath this hope in him purifieth himself, even as he is pure" (1 John 3: 2). Jesus said, "These things have I spoken unto you, that my joy might remain in you, and that your joy might be full" (John 15: 11). "Peace I leave with you, my peace I give unto you" (John 14: 27). "These things I have spoken unto you, that in me ye might have peace. In the world ye shall have tribulation; but be of good cheer; I have overcome the world" (John 16: 33).

They who believe these words of Christ will be partakers of his joy, and will enjoy his peace; and will be of good cheer. They have every reason to do so, knowing that they have an everlasting life, which they can never be deprived of; and knowing that all things work together for their good (Rom. 8: 28), and that all things are now theirs. "For all things are yours; whether Paul, or Apollos, or Cephas, or the world, or life, or death, or things present, or things to come; all are yours; and ye are Christ's; and Christ is God's" (1 Cor. 3: 21).

We are told that the Ethiopian eunuch, after having the fifty-third chapter of Isaiah explained to him, and Jesus preached to him, " said I believe that Jesus Christ is the Son of God," and was baptized; "And he went on his way rejoicing" (Acts 8: 27-39). The jailer at Philippi a few minutes after he was about to kill himself, asked Paul and Silas, "What must I do to be saved; and they said, believe on the Lord Jesus Christ, and thou shalt be saved, thou and thy house. And they spake unto him the word of the Lord, and to all that were in his house. And he took them the same hour of the night, and washed their stripes; and was baptized, he and all his, straightway. And when he had brought them into his house, he set meat before them, and rejoiced, believing in God with all his house" (Acts 16: 27). When a person receives the Lord Jesus Christ, and believes in His name, he realizes that he is saved, and is a child of God, and he will at once rejoice, and try to make others partakers of the joy, and peace, and the good cheer, which Christ gives to all who believe in him. We are told, "Rejoice evermore" (1 Thess. 5: 16). "Rejoice in the Lord always: and again I say, Rejoice" (Phil. 4: 4). "For the joy of the Lord is your strength" (Neh. 8: 10). "Behold, God is my salvation; I will trust, and not be afraid; for the LORD JEHOVAH is my strength and my song; He also has become my salvation. Therefore with joy shall we draw water out of the wells of salvation" (Isaiah 12: 2).

The believer in the Lord Jesus Christ should know that he is saved and hath an eternal life now. Without knowing this he cannot have that joy and peace which come with faith in the Lord Jesus Christ. He cannot bear proper testimony for Christ, and cannot bring others to Him to be saved. "Whosever believeth that Jesus is the Christ is born of God." * * * "He that believeth not God hath made Him a liar; because he believeth not the record, that God gave of His Son. And this is the record that God hath given to us: eternal life, and this life is in His Son. He that hath the Son hath life; and he that hath not the Son of God hath not life. These things have I written unto you that believe on the name of the Son of God; that ye may know that ye have eternal life, and that ye may believe on the name of the Son of God" (1 John 5: 1, 10).

WITNESSES FOR CHRIST.

The first cry of the new-born infant is generally of distress; the first exclamation of the child of God is of joy. This was the case with the Ethiopian eunuch and of the jailer at Philippi, Acts 8: 39; 16: 34. As he grows in grace and knowledge of the Lord Jesus Christ, he will continually rejoice; even in trials and tribulations. "Rejoicing that they were worthy to suffer shame for his name" (Acts 5: 41). "Rejoicing in hope, patient in tribulation" (Rom. 12: 12). "As sorrowful yet always rejoicing" (II Cor. 6: 10; Heb. 3: 6). He also begins to bear witness for Christ: and to spread the knowledge of Him and His salvation; trying thus to save others. The Lord Jesus directs them to do this. "Go ye therefore, and make disciples of all the nations, baptizing them into the name of the Father, and of the Son, and of the Holy Ghost: teaching them to observe all things whatsoever I commanded you: and lo, I am with you always, even unto the end of the world" (Matt. 28: 19). "Sanctify them in the truth; thy word is truth. As thou didst send me into the world, even so sent I them into the world" (John 17: 17).

The children of God need no injunctions to this. They are moved by gratitude and love, as well as by His spirit. Thus we find, that those cured by Jesus could not be restrained from showing their joy, and testifying what Jesus had done for them. The leper cleansed, "went out, and began to publish it much and to blase abroad the matter" (Mark 1: 45). The two blind men whose eyes Jesus opened, "when they were departed, spread abroad His fame in all that country" (Matt. 9: 31). The deaf man with an impediment in his speech, when his ears were opened, and the string of his tongue was loosed, though charged to tell no man; "but the more He charged them, so much the more a great deal they published it" (Mark 7: 36). The woman healed of her infirmity, "immediately she was made straight, and glorified God" (Luke 13: 13). The man born blind, whose eyes Jesus anointed, said, "I went and washed and I received my sight." "One thing I know that, whereas I was blind, now I see" (John 9: 11, 25). The saved will bear testimony for Jesus in Heaven; "Unto Him that loved us, and washed us from our sins in his own blood, and hath made us kings and priests unto God and His Father; to Him be glory and dominion forever and ever. Amen" (Rev. 1: 5).

The saved will also try to bring others to Jesus. John the Baptist said, "Behold the Lamb of God, which taketh away the sin of the world" (John 1: 29). Andrew "first findeth his own brother Simon, and saith unto him, we have found the Messias, which is, being interpreted, the Christ" (John 1: 41). Philip findeth Nathaniel, and said unto him, we have found him of whom Moses in the law, and the prophets, did write, Jesus of Nazareth" (John 1: 45). The disciples scattered abroad, by the persecution of the church, after the stoning of Stephen, " went everywhere preaching the Word." "And the hand of the Lord was with them; and a great number believed, and turned unto the Lord" (Acts 8: 4; 11: 19). These were not duly appointed ministers, or missionaries; but believers scattered by persecution; and wherever they went they talked about the glad tidings of Christ; and the Lord was with them: and a great number believed and turned unto the Lord.

Before His ascension Jesus told his disciples, "Ye shall receive power after the Holy Ghost is come upon you: and ye shall be witnesses unto Me both at Jerusalem, and in all Judea, and in Samaria, and unto the uttermost part of the earth" (Acts 1: 8). Every child of God is a witness for Christ, wherever he may be. He is not only so by talking of Christ, and telling men the Gospel or glad tidings, but is in his life and conversation a living epistle, " known and read of all men; forasmuch as ye are manifestly declared to be the epistle of Christ ministered by us, written not with ink but with the Spirit of the living God; not in tables of stone, but in fleshly tables of the head" (II Cor. 3: 2). With Paul he will say,

"Christ shall be magnified in my body, whether it be by life, or by death. For to me to live is Christ, and to die is gain" (Phil. 1: 20).

THE CHILDREN OF GOD MUST GROW.

A child who does not grow in knowledge is virtually dead. True life in man combines health, growth, activity and happiness. The Christian who does not grow in grace and in the knowledge of our Lord and Saviour Jesus Christ, is likewise virtually dead. "Faith if it have not works is dead" (James 2: 17). The barren fig tree will be cut down. "Every branch in me that beareth not fruit, he taketh away" (John 15: 2). A branch that does not grow cannot bear fruit. Joined to Christ, as the branch is to the vine, and drawing life from Him, we will be constantly growing, and bearing fruit to the glory of God. A child of God, when born of the Spirit, has passed from death to everlasting life. His sins are atoned for. "As far as the east is from the west, so far hath he removed our transgressions from us" (Psm. 103: 3, 12). "Being justified by faith, we have peace with God through our Lord Jesus Christ" (Rom. 5; 1). But he is a child just beginning to live. He is saved, but he must work out the salvation he has received; remembering that it is God who worketh in him both to will and to do. Saved by the grace of God he has to grow in grace and in the knowledge of Christ continually. Peter closes his epistles with, "Ye therefore, beloved, seeing ye know these things before, beware lest ye also, being led away with the error of the wicked, fall from your own steadfastness. But grow in grace, and in the knowledge of our Lord and Saviour Jesus Christ. To Him be glory both now and for ever. Amen" (II Peter 3: 18). Men have lost the knowledge of God, "and even as they did not like to retain God in their knowledge, God gave them over to a reprobate mind, to do those things which are not convenient; being filled with all unrighteousness, fornication, wickedness, covetousness," &c., &c. (Rom. 1: 28-31). We must grow in the knowledge of God in Christ. In His prayer for His disciples, and for those who shall believe on Him through their word, in the 17th chapter of John, Jesus said, "Father, the hour has come; glorify Thy Son, that Thy Son also may glorify Thee: as Thou hast given Him power over all flesh, that He should give eternal life to as many as Thou hast given Him. And this is life eternal, that they might know Thee, the only true God, and Jesus Christ, whom Thou hast sent" (John 17: 1). He had before told them, "All things are delivered to Me of My Father; and no man knoweth who the Son is, but the Father; and who the Father is, but the Son, and he to whom the Son will reveal Him" (Luke 10: 22). The children of God who have received this revelation, and have eternal life, are therefore told to grow in grace and in the knowledge of the Lord Jesus

Christ. Peter tells them how they are to grow. "As new-born babes, desire the sincere milk of the word, that ye may grow thereby" (I Pet. 2: 2). Paul writing to the "Sanctified in Christ Jesus, called saints," in Corinth, addresses them "as babes in Christ," and says, "I have fed you with milk, and not with meat; for hitherto ye were not able to bear it, neither yet are ye able, for ye are carnal" (I Cor. 3: 2). In the Epistle to the Hebrews it is written, "For when for the time ye ought to be teachers, ye have need that one teach you again which be the first principles of the oracles of God; and are become such as have need of milk, and not of strong meat. For every one that useth milk is unskillful in the word of righteousness: for he is a babe" (Heb. 5: 12).

Paul with all his revelations, and though sure that he was saved, and had everlasting life, and that for him to die was gain, to depart was to be with Christ, writes, "Brethren, I count not myself to have apprehended: but this one thing I do, forgetting those things which are behind, and reaching forth unto those things which are before, I press toward the mark for the prize of the high calling of God in Christ Jesus" (Phil. 3: 8–14). Jesus prayed, "Sanctify them through Thy truth: Thy Word is truth" (John 17: 17). The new-born child of God will continue to grow forever.

Paul and Timotheus writing to the saints and faithful brethren in Christ which are at Colasse say, "We do not cease to pray for you, and to desire that ye might be filled with the knowledge of His will in all wisdom and spiritual understanding; that ye might walk worthy of the Lord unto all pleasing, being fruitful in every good work, and increasing in the knowledge of God; strengthened with all might, according to His glorious power, unto all patience and long suffering with joyfulness; giving thanks unto the Father, who hath made us meet to be partakers of the inheritance of the saints in light: who hath delivered from the power of darkness, and hath translated us into the kingdom of His dear Son: in whom we have redemption through His blood, even the forgiveness of sins" (Col. 1: 9).

The whole Bible is a revelation of the Lord Jesus Christ. To grow in grace and the knowledge of Him, we must know the Scriptures. To know them, we must study them and feed upon them; and see Christ in them from the beginning to the end. We must receive Him, as He is revealed in them; for the Word is Christ. "In the beginning was the Word, and the Word was with God, and the Word was God. * * * And the Word was made flesh, and dwelt among us, and we beheld His glory, the glory of the only begotten of the Father, full of grace and truth. * * * And of His fulness have all we received, and grace for grace" (John 1: 1, 14, 16). Christ says, "I am the living bread which came down from heaven:

if any man eat of this bread, he shall live forever." * * * "It is the Spirit that quickeneth; the flesh profiteth nothing; the words that I speak unto you, they are Spirit, and they are life" (John 6: 51, 63). As the children of Israel had to gather the manna every day so are we to gather and feed upon the words of Christ, and thus to feed upon Him day by day.

Another way to grow in grace and the knowledge of Christ, and to be a witness for Him, is to be regular in our attendance at the meetings of the church with which we are connected, and to fill our place there. The Word of God tells us, "Let us hold fast the profession of our faith without wavering; (for He is faithful that promised); and let us consider one another to provoke unto love and to good works; not forsaking the assembling of ourselves together, as the manner of some is; but exhorting one another: and so much the more, as ye see the day approaching" (Heb. 10: 23; 3: 13). We need faith in the words of the Lord Jesus Christ. "Again I say unto you, that if two of you shall agree on earth, as touching anything that they shall ask, it shall be done for them of my Father which is in Heaven. For where two or three are gathered together in my name, there am I in the midst of them" (Matt. 18: 19; John 16: 23). If we love Him, we will go where He promises to meet us. If we believe Him, we will be where two or three gather in His name to pray. Every member of the church should take interest in its meetings, and give them the precedence over all other gatherings. Every member, according to the gift of the Spirit, should take part in them. "There are diversities of gifts, but the same Spirit. * * * The manifestation of the Spirit is given to every man to profit withal. * * * For all these worketh the self-same Spirit, dividing to every man severally as He will. For as the body is one, and hath many members, and all the members of that one body, being many, are one body; so also is Christ. For by one Spirit are we all baptized into one body" (I Cor. 12: 4, 7, 11). "How is it then brethren? When ye come together, every one of you hath a psalm, hath a doctrine, hath a tongue, hath a revelation, hath an interpretation. Let all things be done unto edifying. * * * For ye may all prophesy one by one, that all may learn, and all may be comforted" (I Cor. 14: 26, 31). "Wherefore comfort yourselves together, and edify one another, even as also ye do" (I Thess. 5: 11). The Revised Version says, "Wherefore exhort one another, and build each other up, even as also ye do." "Speaking to yourselves in psalms and hymns and spiritual songs, singing and making melody in your heart to the Lord; giving thanks always for all things unto God and the Father in the name of our Lord Jesus Christ" (Eph. 5: 19). "Let the Word of Christ dwell in you richly in all wisdom; teaching and admonishing one another in psalms and hymns and spiritual songs, singing with grace in your hearts to the Lord" (Col. 3: 16). If you want to grow in grace and knowledge, do not neglect the means of grace; "Forsake not the assembling of yourselves together as the manner of some is." We hear members of volunteer military companies boast that they have not missed attending a single weekly drill for years. The believer in the Lord Jesus Christ has much more reason to attend regularly the weekly meetings of His church. That he may grow in grace and knowledge himself, and be fitted to be " a good soldier of Jesus Christ" (II Tim. 2: 3). As the Christian grows in the grace of the Holy Spirit, and the knowledge of Christ, he will not only be increasing his own spiritual joy and peace, but knowing more of Christ, and of His Word, he will be better able to bear testimony for Christ, to bring souls to Him, and to strengthen and comfor His sheep and His lambs.

"Now the God of peace, that brought again from the dead our Lord Jesus, that Great Shepherd of the sheep, through the blood of the everlasting covenant, make you perfect in every good work .to do His will, working in you that which is well pleasing in His sight, through Jesus Christ; to whom be glory forever and ever. Amen" (Heb. 13: 20).

CHILDREN OF GOD

AND

UNION WITH CHRIST

PART II.

UNION WITH CHRIST.

"Abide in me and I in you," "I am the vine, ye are the branches: He that abideth in me, and I in him, the same beareth much fruit; for apart from me ye can do nothing."—John xv: 1-10. "That they all may be one, as thou, Father, art in me, and I in thee, that they also may be one in us," "I in them, and thou in me."—
John xvii: 11, 21, 23, 26.

INDEX.—Part II.

	PAGE
The most important of all knowledge is to know the Lord Jesus Christ	125
The Lord Jesus Christ.—His name—Lord.	137
The Lord Jesus Christ.—His name—Jesus.	144
The Lord Jesus Christ.—His name—Christ.	147
Christ our Anointed Prophet.	150
Christ our Anointed Priest.	159
Union of believers, with Christ, in his death, burial and resurrection	164
Christ our Anointed King	172
Union with Christ—Christ our Life.	182
Union with Christ—Christ our Food	187
Union with Christ—Father, Brother, Friend	202
Union with Christ—Husband and Wife	207
Christ corner-stone, believers living stones built on him	214
Christ and Believers—Shepherd and Sheep.	218
Christ the Head, and believers in Him, members of His body	227
Christ the Vine, believers in Him the branches	234
Union of believers with Christ and the Holy Spirit, and the Father, one in God	248

THE MOST IMPORTANT OF ALL KNOWLEDGE IS TO KNOW THE LORD JESUS CHRIST.

Paul, writing to the saints in Rome, says: "I am not ashamed of the Gospel of Christ: for it is the power of God unto salvation, to every one that believeth; to the Jew first, and also to the Greek" (Rom. 1: 16). Writing to the saints in Christ Jesus, at Philippi, he says, "I count all things but loss, for the excellency of the knowledge of Christ Jesus, my Lord; for whom I have suffered the loss of all things, and do count them but dung, that I may win Christ, and be found in Him, not having mine own righteousness, which is of the law, but that which is through the faith of Christ, the righteousness which is of God by faith: that I may know Him" (Phil. 3: 8). In his prayer for his disciples, Jesus said, "This is life eternal, that they might know Thee, the only true God, and Jesus Christ, whom Thou hast sent" (John 17: 3). "Jesus saith unto Thomas, I am the way, and the truth, and the life: no man cometh unto the Father but by me. If ye had known me, ye should have known my Father also: and from henceforth ye know Him, and have seen Him" (John 14: 6). In the first chapter of First Corinthians, Paul brings the name of Christ in seventeen times; it appears in almost every verse. He then says, "And I, brethren, when I came to you, came not with excellency of speech or of wisdom, declaring unto you the testimony of God. For I determined not to know anything among you, save Jesus Christ, and Him crucified" (1 Cor. 2: 1).

The following to the end of this chapter is an extract from "The Fountain of Life," by Rev. John Flavel, A.D. 1671 (*American Tract Society*). It is the introductory chapter, showing the importance of the knowledge of Christ.

"The excellency of the subject.

"*For I determined not to know any thing among you, save Jesus Christ, and Him crucified.*"—1 Cor. 2: 2.

The former verse contains an apology for the plain and familiar manner of the apostle's preaching, which was "not with the excellency of speech, or of wisdom:" he studied not to gratify their curiosity with rhetorical strains, or philosophical niceties; for he says, "I determined not to know any thing among you, save Jesus Christ, and Him crucified."

"*I determined not to know.*" The meaning is not, that he despised or contemned all other knowledge, but so far only as it might stand in competition with, or opposition to the knowledge of Jesus Christ. As if he had said, "It is my stated, settled judgment; not a hasty, inconsiderate censure, but the result of my most serious inquiries. After I have well weighed the case, viewed it exactly on every side, balanced all advantages and disadvantages, pondered all things that are fit to come into consideration about it; this is the issue and final determination, that all other knowledge, how profitable, how pleasant soever, is not worthy to be named in comparison with the knowledge of Jesus Christ. This, therefore, I resolve to make the scope and end of my ministry, and the end regulates the means; such pedantic toys and airy notions as injudicious ears affect, would rather obstruct than promote my grand design among you; therefore, wholly waving that way, I applied myself to a plain, popular, unaffected dialect, fitted rather to pierce the heart and convince the conscience, than to please the fancy.

"'*I determined not to know any thing*'—to study nothing myself, to teach nothing to you, but 'Jesus Christ.' Christ shall be the centre to which all the lines of my ministry shall be drawn. I have spoken and written of many other subjects in my sermons and epistles, but it is all as consequent upon preaching and making known Jesus Christ: of all the subjects in the world, this is the sweetest; if there be anything, on this side of heaven, worthy our time and studies, this is it. Thus he magnifies his doctrine, from the excellency of its subject, accounting all other doctrines but airy things, compared with this.

"Jesus Christ and *Him crucified.*" This topic he singled out from all the rest of the excellent truths of Christ, on which to spend the main strength of his ministry: Christ *as crucified:* and the rather, because hereby he would obviate the vulgar prejudice raised against Him upon the account of His cross; for Christ crucified was "to the Jews a stumbling-block, and to the Greeks, foolishness." 1 Cor. 1: 23. This also best suited his end, to draw them on to Christ; as Christ above all other subjects, so Christ crucified above all things in Christ.

The manner in which he discoursed on this transcendent subject to them, is also remarkable; he not only preached Christ crucified, but he preached Him assiduously and *plainly.* He preached Christ frequently; "and whenever he preached of Christ crucified, he preached Him in a crucified style." This is the sum of the words; to let them know that his spirit was intent upon this subject, as if he neither knew nor cared to speak of any other. All his sermons were so full of Christ, that hearers might have thought he was acquainted with no other doctrine. Hence,

No doctrine is more excellent, or necessary to be preached and studied, than Jesus Christ, and Him crucified.

All other knowledge, how much soever it be magnified in the world, is, and ought to be, esteemed but dross, in comparison with the excellency of the knowledge of Jesus Christ.

Phil. 3: 8. "In whom are hid all the treasures of wisdom and knowledge." Col. 2: 3.

Eudoxus was so affected with the glory of the sun, that he thought he was born only to behold it: much more should a Christian judge himself born only to behold and delight in the glory of the Lord Jesus.

I. Consider the excellency of the knowledge of Christ *in itself*.

1. It is *the very marrow and kernel of all the Scriptures;* the scope and centre of all divine revelations. The ceremonial law is full of Christ, and all the Gospel is full of Christ: the blessed lines of both Testaments meet in Him; and how they both harmonize, and sweetly concentre in Jesus Christ, it is the chief scope of the excellent epistle to the Hebrews to unfold; for we may call that epistle the sweet harmony of both Testaments.

This argues the unspeakable excellency of this doctrine, the knowledge whereof must needs, therefore, be a key to unlock the greatest part of the sacred Scriptures. For it is in the understanding of Scripture, much as in the knowledge of logic and philosophy: if a scholar once come to understand the foundation—principle, upon which, as upon its hinge, the controversy turns, the true knowledge of that principle shall carry him through the whole controversy, and furnish him with a solution to every argument.

Even so the right knowledge of Jesus Christ,

like a clue, leads you through the whole labyrinth of the Scriptures.

2. The knowledge of Jesus Christ is a *fundamental knowledge;* and foundations are most useful, though least seen.

It is fundamental to all *graces;* they all begin in knowledge. "The new man is renewed in knowledge." Col. 3: 10. As the old, so the new creation begins in light; the opening of the eyes is the first work of the Spirit: and as the beginnings of grace, so all its growth depends upon this increasing knowledge; "But grow in grace, and in the knowledge of our Lord and Saviour." 2 Pet. 3: 18. See how these two, grace and knowledge, keep equal pace in the soul of a Christian; in what degree the one increases the other increases also.

It is fundamental to all *duties.* The duties, as well as the graces of all Christians, are all founded in the knowledge of Christ.

Must a Christian believe? That he can never do without the knowledge of Christ: faith is so much dependent on his knowledge, that it is denominated by it; "By His knowledge shall my righteous servant justify many," Isa. 53: 11; and hence, in John 6: 40, seeing and believing are made the same thing. Would a man exercise hope in God? That he can never do withont the knowledge of Christ, for He is the author of that hope, 1 Pet. 1: 3; He is also its object, Heb. 6: 19; its groundwork and support, Col. 1: 27. And as you cannot believe or hope, so neither can you pray acceptably without a competent degree of this knowledge. The very heathen could say, "Men must not speak of God without light." The true way of conversing with, and enjoying God in prayer, is by acting faith on Him through a Mediator. Oh, then, how indispensable is the knowledge of Christ to all who address themselves to God in any duty!

It is fundamental to all *comforts:* all the comforts of believers are streams from this fountain. Jesus Christ is the very object of a believer's joy; "We rejoice in Christ Jesus." Phil. 3: 3. Take away the knowledge of Christ, and Christians would be the most sad and melancholy beings in the world: again, let Christ but manifest Himself, and dart the beams of His light into their souls, it will make them kiss the stake, sing in the flames, and shout in the pangs of death, as men that divide the spoil.

This knowledge is fundamental to the *eternal happiness* of souls: as we can perform no duty, enjoy no comfort, so neither can we be saved without it, "This is life eternal, that they might know Thee the only true God, and Jesus Christ, whom Thou hast sent." John 17: 3.

And if it be life eternal to know Christ, then it is eternal damnation to be ignorant of Christ: as Christ is the door that opens heaven, so knowledge is the key that opens Christ. The excellent gifts and renowned parts of the moral heathen, though they purchased to them great esteem and honor among men, yet left them in a state of perdition, because of this great defect, that they were ignorant of Christ. 1 Cor. 1: 21.

3. The knowledge of Christ is *profound and large:* all other sciences are but shadows; this is a boundless, bottomless ocean; no creature hath a line long enough to fathom the depth of it; there is height, length, depth, and breadth ascribed to it, Eph. 3: 18; yea, it passeth knowledge. There is a manifold wisdom of God in Christ. Eph. 3: 10. It is indeed simple, pure, and unmixed with any thing but itself, yet is manifold in degrees, kinds, and administrations Though something of Christ be unfolded in one age, and something in another, yet eternity itself cannot fully unfold Him. I see something, said Luther, which blessed Augustine saw not; and those that come after me, will see that which I see not. It is in the studying of Christ, as in the planting of a new-discovered country; at first men sit down by the sea-side, upon the skirts and borders of the land, and there they dwell; but by degrees they search further and further into the heart of the country. Ah, the best of us are yet but upon the borders of this vast continent!

4. The study of Jesus Christ is *the most noble subject* that ever a soul spent itself upon. The angels study this doctrine, and stoop down to look into this deep abyss. What are the truths

discovered in Christ, but the very secrets that from eternity lay hid in the bosom of God? Eph. 3: 8, 9. God's heart is opened to men in Christ, John 1: 18; this makes the Gospel such a glorious dispensation, because Christ is so gloriously revealed therein, 2 Cor. 3: 9; and the studying of Christ in the Gospel, stamps such a heavenly glory upon the contemplating soul. Verse 18.

5. It is the most *sweet and comfortable knowledge.* To be studying Jesus Christ, what is it but to be digging among all the veins and springs of comfort? and the deeper you dig, the more do these springs flow upon you. How are hearts enraptured with the discoveries of Christ in the Gospel! what ecstasies, meltings, transports, do gracious souls meet there!

II. Let us *compare* this knowledge with all other knowledge.

1. All other knowledge is natural, but this wholly *supernatural*, "No man knoweth the Son, but the Father; neither knoweth any the Father, save the Son, and he to whom soever the Son will reveal Him." Matt. 11: 27. The wisest heathen could never make a discovery of Christ by their deepest searches into nature; the most eagle-eyed philosophers were but children in knowledge compared with the most illiterate Christians.

2. Other knowledge is *unattainable by many.* All the helps and means in the world would never enable some Christians to attain the

learned arts and languages; men of the brightest parts are most excellent in these; but here is the mystery and excellency of the knowledge of Christ, that men of most blunt, dull, and contemptible parts attain, through the teaching of the Spirit, to this knowledge, in which the more acute and ingenious are utterly blind: "I thank Thee, O Father, Lord of heaven and earth, because Thou hast hid these things from the wise and prudent, and hast revealed them unto babes." Matt. 11: 25. "Ye see your calling, brethren, how that not many wise men after the flesh, not many mighty, not many noble, are called: but God hath chosen the foolish things of the world to confound the wise." 1 Cor. 1: 26, 27.

3. Other knowledge, though you should attain the highest degree of it, would *never bring you to heaven.* The principal thing, namely Christ, being wanting. Other knowledge is also defective, in the purity of its nature: the learned heathens grew vain in their imaginations, Rom. 1: 21; and in its efficacy and influence on the heart and life: they held the truth in unrighteousness: their lusts were stronger than their light, Rom. 1: 18. But this knowledge has most powerful influences, changing souls into its own image, 2 Cor. 3: 18, and so proves a saving knowledge unto men. 1 Tim. 2: 4.

Inference 1. The sufficiency of the doctrine of Christ, to make men *wise unto salvation.*

Paul desired to know nothing else; and, indeed, nothing else is of absolute necessity to be known. A little of this knowledge, if saving and effectual upon thy heart, will do the soul more service than all the vain speculation and profound parts in which others so much glory.

Poor Christian, be not dejected, because thou seest thyself outstript and excelled by so many in other parts of knowledge; if thou know Jesus Christ, thou knowest enough to comfort and save thy soul. Many learned philosophers are now in hell, and many illiterate Christians in heaven.

This may inform us *by what rule to judge* both ministers and doctrine. Certainly that is the highest commendation of a minister, to be " an able minister of the New Testament; not of the letter, but of the spirit." 2 Cor. 3: 6. He is the best preacher, that can in the most lively and powerful manner, display Jesus Christ before the people, evidently setting Him forth as crucified among them; and that is the best sermon which is most full of Christ, not of rhetorical art.

I know that a holy dialect well becometh Christ's ministers; they should not be rude or careless in language or method; but surely the excellency of a sermon lies not in that, but in the plainest exhibition and liveliest application of Jesus Christ.

Let all that mind the honor of religion, or the peace and comfort of their own souls, wholly *apply themselves to the study* of Jesus Christ, and Him crucified.

As to the *people* that sit under the doctrine of Christ daily, and have the light of His knowledge shining round about them: take heed ye do not reject and despise this light.

This may be done by neglecting the means of knowledge. Surely, if you thus reject knowledge, God will reject you. Hos. 4: 6.

Take heed also that you rest not satisfied with that knowledge of Christ you have attained, but *go on to perfection*

THE LORD JESUS CHRIST. HIS NAME, LORD.

In the Scriptures great stress is laid on the name of God. Each different name ascribed to Him reveals Him. In the Bible, God thus reveals Himself, by many different names; such as, Father, Husband, Saviour, The God of all Grace, The God of Patience and Consolation, The God of Hope, The God of Peace, etc, etc. The Lord Jesus Christ likewise reveals Himself to us in the Scriptures by the use of very many names. When God sent Moses to deliver the children of Israel, Moses said unto God, "Behold, when I come unto the children of Israel, and shall say unto them, The God of your fathers hath sent me unto you; and they shall say to me, What is His name? what shall I say unto them? And God said unto Moses, I am that I am: and He said, Thus shalt thou say unto the children of Israel, I Am hath sent me unto you. And God said moreover unto Moses, The Jehovah, God of your fathers, the God of Abraham, the God of Isaac, and the God of Jacob, hath sent me unto you: this is my name forever, and this is my memorial unto all generations" (Exod. 3: 13). The Lord Jesus refers to this name, "I am the God of Abraham," etc., in proof of the resurrection (Matt. 22: 32; Mark

12: 27; Luke 20: 37). His name JEHOVAH, I AM, appears very frequently in the Old Testament, especially in the Psalms. That name of God was held in such reverence by the Jews, that in reading the Scriptures, they would not pronounce it, but would put another word in its place. In our Bible, the translators have done the same. Wherever the word LORD appears in capitals in the Old Testament, in the original it is JEHOVAH. This name is far more impressive, and far more expressive, and it should have been retained. In the ten commandments, a special commandment is, That His name is to be held in reverence, and not to be taken in vain. The Lord's prayer begins with "Hallowed be Thy name." David exclaims, "Bless Jehovah, O my soul: and all that is within, bless His holy name. Bless Jehovah, O my soul, and forget not all His benefits: who forgiveth all thine iniquities; who healeth all thy diseases; who redeemeth thy life from destruction; who crowneth thee with loving kindness and tender mercies; who satisfieth thy mouth with good things; so that thy youth is renewed like the eagle's" (Psm. 103: 1).

Among the predictions in Isaiah of the coming of the Lord Jesus Christ, some of them refer to His name, and to His being God. "Behold, a virgin shall conceive, and bear a Son, and shall call His name Immanuel" (Isai. 7: 14). This is quoted at the birth of Christ, "And they shall call His name Immanuel, which being interpreted is, God with us" (Matt. 1: 23). "For unto us a child is born, unto us a Son is given: and the government shall be on His shoulder: and His name shall be called Wonderful, Counsellor, The Mighty God, The Everlasting Father, The Prince of Peace. Of the increase of His government and peace, there shall be no end" (Isai. 9: 6). The names and attributes of God are here ascribed to the Lord Jesus Christ. Paul, writing to Timothy, says: "Without controversy, great is the mystery of godliness: God was manifest in the flesh, justified in the Spirit, seen of angels, preached unto the Gentiles, believed on in the world, received up into glory" (1 Tim. 3: 16). To the church in Corinth he writes: "All things are of God, who hath reconciled us to Himself by Jesus Christ, and hath given to us the ministry of reconciliation; to wit, that God was in Christ, reconciling the world unto Himself, not imputing their trespasses unto them" (2 Cor. 5: 18). Jesus asserts this, when He says, "I and my Father are one" (John 10: 30). "The Father is in me, and I in Him" (John 10: 38). "Verily, verily, I say unto you, before Abraham was, I am" (John 8: 58). "Where two or three are gathered together in my name, there am I in the midst of them" (Matt. 18: 20). "Lo, I am with you alway, even unto the end of the world" (Matt. 28: 20). To do this, He must be omnipotent. omniscient and omnipresent.

The children of God are to be baptized "in

the name of the Father, and of the Son, and of the Holy Ghost" (Matt. 28: 31)—not names, but one name; one God.

Speaking of the Lord Jesus Christ, the Scriptures tell us, "He was in the world, and the world was made by Him; and the world knew Him not. He came unto His own, and His own received Him not. But as many as received Him, to them gave He the right to become children of God, even to them that believe on His name: which were born, not of blood, nor of the will of the flesh, nor of the will of man, but of God" (John 1: 10). We cannot "receive Christ," unless "we believe on His name." We cannot believe in Him, unless we believe in his name. Peter, speaking to the Jews, after healing the man lame from his mother's womb, who was made to walk and leap, said: "Ye denied the Holy One, and the Just, and desired a murderer to be granted unto you; and killed the Prince of Life, whom God hath raised from the dead; whereof we are witnesses. And His name, through faith in his name, hath made this man strong, whom ye see and know: yea, the faith which is by him hath given him this perfect soundness in the presence of you all" (Acts 3: 15). They who "believe on His name" become children of God, and by "faith in His name" are made "strong," and receive "perfect soundness." "But he that believeth not is condemned already, because he hath not believed in the name of the only begotten Son of God" (John 3: 18, 36). Again and again Christ says, "Whatsoever ye shall ask in my name, that will I do, that the Father may be glorified in the Son. If ye ask anything in my name, I will do it" (John 14: 13). "Verily, verily, I say unto you, whatsoever ye shall ask the Father in my name, He will give it you. Hitherto have ye asked nothing in my name. Ask, and ye shall receive, that your joy may be full" (John 16: 23). His name, His whole name, "THE LORD JESUS CHRIST," we must believe in; must receive; must be saved by; and must grow in the knowledge of. (Acts 11: 17; 15: 11; 16: 31; 20: 21; Rom. 5: 1, 11; 6: 23; 8: 39; 16: 20; 2 Cor. 13: 14; Gal. 6: 18; 2 Thess. 3: 18; 1 Cor. 15: 57; 2 Cor. 1: 2; 2 Pet. 3: 18).

In the Scriptures, the creation of the worlds, and what is called providence, are ascribed to the Lord Jesus Christ. "To us there is but one God, the Father, of whom are all things, and we in Him; and one Lord Jesus Christ, by whom are all things, and we by Him" (1 Cor. 8: 6). "God, who at sundry times and in divers manners spake in time past unto the fathers by the prophets, hath in these last days spoken unto us by His Son, whom He hath appointed heir of all things, by whom also He made the worlds; who being the brightness of His glory, and the express image of His person, and upholding all things by the word of His power, when He had by Himself purged our sins, sat down on the right hand of the Majesty on high" (Heb. 1: 1). "In whom we have redemption through His blood, even the forgiveness of sins; who is the image of the invisible God, the first born of every creature; for by Him were all things created, that are in heaven, and that are in earth, visible and invisible, whether they be thrones, or dominions, or principalities, or powers: all things were created by Him, and for Him: and He is before all things, and by Him all things consist: and He is the head of the body, the church: who is the beginning, the first born from the dead; that in all things He might have the preeminence. For it pleased the Father that in Him should all fulness dwell; and having made peace through the blood of His cross, by Him to reconcile all things unto Himself" (Col. 1: 14). "Let this mind be in you, which was also in Christ Jesus: who, being in the form of God, thought it not robbery to be equal with God: but made Himself of no reputation, and took upon Him the form of a servant, and was made in the likeness of men: and being found in fashion as a man, He humbled Himself, and became obedient unto death, even the death of the cross. Wherefore God also hath highly exalted Him, and given Him a name which is above every name: that at the name of Jesus every knee should bow, of things in heaven, and things in earth, and things under the earth; and that every tongue should confess that Jesus

Christ is Lord, to the glory of God, the Father" (Phil. 2: 5).

Jesus Christ as Lord is to be preached. Paul says, "If our gospel be hid, it is hid to them that are lost: in whom the god of this world hath blinded the minds of them which believe not, lest the light of the glorious gospel of Christ, who is the image of God, should shine unto them. For we preach not ourselves, but Christ Jesus, the Lord" (2 Cor. 4: 5). We are also told, "The word is nigh thee, even in thy mouth, and in thy heart: that is the word of faith, which we preach; that if thou shalt confess with thy mouth the Lord Jesus, and shalt believe in thine heart that God hath raised Him from the dead, thou shalt be saved" (Rom. 10: 9). "For whosoever shall call upon the name of the Lord shall be saved" (Rom. 10: 13). If we do not believe in Him as The Lord, Jehovah, The I Am; "Jesus Christ, the same yesterday, and to-day, and forever" (Heb. 13: 8), our faith is vain, we are yet in our sins. Believing in Him as the LORD, we can trust in Him as the Jesus, and as the Christ. We are sure that what we ask of the Father in His name, He will do it, for all power is His, in heaven and in earth (Matt. 28: 18; John 14: 13; 16: 23).

THE LORD JESUS CHRIST. HIS NAME, JESUS.

The name of the Lord Jesus Christ signifies His person, His authority, and His work. Unless He was the Lord, He could not be Jesus, Saviour. No creature could have atoned for the sin of man; no creature could have redeemed Him. As Jesus Christ, He is "The same yesterday, and to-day, and forever" (Heb. 13: 8). His name, Jesus, is the Greek form of the Hebrew, Joshua, which means Jehovah saves, or Saviour. He is spoken of as Jesus in the Bible 711 times. The name Jesus was given to him before his birth. Mary was told by the angel that she should bring forth a Son, and "shalt call His name Jesus. He shall be great, and shall be called the Son of the Highest" (Luke 1: 31). To her husband, Joseph, the angel of the Lord said, "That which is conceived in her is of the Holy Ghost. And she shall bring forth a Son, and thou shalt call His name Jesus: for He shall save His people from their sins" (Matt. 1: 21). When Jesus was born, the angel of the Lord came upon the shepherds, and the glory of the Lord shone round about them, and the angel said unto them, "Behold, I bring good tidings of great joy, which shall be to all people. For unto you is born this day, in the city of David, a Saviour, which is Christ the Lord" (Luke 2: 11). The children of God receive the Lord Jesus Christ, and believe in His name, not only as the LORD, but also as JESUS, their Saviour. Not merely as an example, not as a helper, but as their Saviour. Looking away from everything else, they look unto Jesus as "The author and perfecter of their faith" (Heb. 12: 1). They may well do this, "for there is none other name under heaven given among men, whereby we must be saved" (Acts 4: 12). The whole Bible, from the sacrifice of Abel, in Genesis, to the Lamb in the midst of the throne, reveals Jesus as the only Saviour. "Surely He hath borne our griefs, and carried our sorrows. * * * But he was wounded for our transgressions, He was bruised for our iniquities: the chastisement of our peace was upon Him; and with His stripes we are healed. All we like sheep have gone astray; we have turned every one to his own way; and the Lord hath laid on Him the iniquity of us all" (Isai. 53: 4). "Christ also suffered for us, * * * who His own self bare our sins in His own body on the tree, that we, being dead to sins, should live unto righteousness: by whose stripes ye were healed" (1 Peter 2: 21, 24). "For He hath made Him to be sin for us, who knew no sin; that we might be made the righteousness of God in Him" (2 Cor. 5: 21). The believer realizes that "Christ, our passover, is sacrificed for us' (1 Cor. 5: 7), and "after He had offered one sacrifice for sins forever, sat down on the right hand of God; from henceforth expecting, till His enemies be made His footstool. For by one offering He hath perfected forever them that are sanctified" (Heb. 10: 12): and, rejoicing in Christ's words, that, believing in Him, he has everlasting life (John 3: 31), and is saved, he is ready to take up the song here, "Unto Him that loved us, and washed us from our sins in His own blood, and hath made us kings and priests unto God and His Father, to Him be glory and dominion, for ever and ever. Amen" (Rev. 1: 5).

THE LORD JESUS CHRIST. HIS NAME, CHRIST.

To ACCOMPLISH the work of saving men, which the LORD undertook, it was necessary that He should become, JESUS; and also, CHRIST. The word Christ is from the Greek, and corresponds with the word Messiah in the Hebrew. The meaning of it is, Anointed. Christ is the official name of the Lord Jesus. We cannot receive Him, and believe in Him, without believing in Him as The Christ. Anointed of God with the Holy Spirit, as our Prophet, our Priest, and our King. In the Old Testament, those appointed by God to hold these offices were anointed, as types of the coming Messiah. Isaiah, writing of the coming Christ, and of His anointing, says, "The Spirit of the Lord God is upon me; because Jehovah hath anointed me to preach good tidings unto the meek; He hath sent me to bind up the broken-hearted, to proclaim liberty to the captives, and the opening of the prison to them that are bound; to proclaim the acceptable year of Jehovah, and the day of vengeance of our God; to comfort all that mourn; to appoint unto them that mourn in Zion, to give unto them beauty for ashes, the oil of joy for mourning, the garment of praise for the spirit of heaviness; that they might be called trees of righteousness, the planting of Jehovah, that He might be glorified" (Isai. 61: 1). At the commencement of His ministry, Jesus applied this passage to Himself, saying, "This day is this Scripture fulfilled in your eyes" (Luke 4: 21). "God anointed Jesus of Nazareth with the Holy Ghost, and with power: who went about doing good, and healing all that were oppressed of the devil, for God was with Him" (Acts 10: 38). "And John bare record, saying, I saw the Spirit descending from heaven like a dove, and it abode upon Him, and I knew Him not; but He that sent me to baptize with water, the same said unto me, Upon whom thou shalt see the Spirit descending, and remaining on Him, the same is He which baptizeth with the Holy Ghost. And I saw, and bare record, that this is the Son of God. Again, the next day after, John stood, and two of his disciples; and looking upon Jesus as He walked, he saith, Behold the Lamb of God! * * * One of the two which heard John speak, and followed him, was Andrew, Simon Peter's brother. He first findeth his own brother, Simon, and saith unto him, We have found the Messias, which is, being interpreted, the Christ" (John 1: 32, 41).

Faith in Him, as the Christ, is the test question with every creed, and with every individual. Jesus asked the Pharisees, "What think ye of Christ? Whose Son is He? He also saith unto His disciples, But whom say ye that I am? And Simon Peter answered and said, Thou art the Christ, the Son of the living God" (Matt. 16: 15). Our Lord's reply is applicable to all believers in Him. "And Jesus answered and said unto him, Blessed art thou, Simon Barjona: for flesh and blood hath not revealed it unto thee, but my Father, which is in heaven" (Matt. 16: 17). We are elsewhere told, "Whosoever believeth that Jesus is the Christ, is born of God" (1 John 5: 1). The Lord Jesus is to be preached to men as, "The Christ, the Son of the living God." On this rock, Christ said, I will build my church, and the gates of hell shall not prevail against it. Paul says, "For I determined not to know anything among you save Jesus Christ, and Him crucified" (1 Cor. 2: 2). "For other foundation can no man lay than that is laid, which is Jesus Christ." Let every man take heed how he buildeth thereupon" (1 Cor. 3: 10) Isaiah foretold this. "Thus saith the Lord God, Behold, I lay in Zion for a foundation a stone, a tried stone, a precious corner stone, a sure foundation: he that believeth shall not make haste" (Isai. 28: 16). "To whom coming, as unto a living stone, disallowed indeed of men, but chosen of God, and precious, ye also, as lively stones, are built up a spiritual house, an holy priesthood, to offer up spiritual sacrifices, acceptable to God by Jesus Christ" (1 Pet. 2: 4).

CHRIST, OUR ANOINTED PROPHET.

The history of the Jews, from the call of Abraham, is a pictorial lesson which should be studied. It presents a continued series of types. The covenant made by God with Abraham and his seed, which has continued nearly four thousand years, until the present day; the deliverance of the Jews from Egypt; their journey through the wilderness, under the guidance of Moses, fed daily with bread from heaven; their miraculous deliverances from their enemies; their being carried into captivity to Babylon; and their ultimate dispersion through all nations because of their forsaking God; their mode of worship, sacrifices, priesthood and temple, all were types; and are object-lessons which should be well understood. They "did all eat the same spiritual meat, and did all drink the same spiritual drink; for they drank of that spiritual Rock that followed them: and that Rock was Christ" (1 Cor. 10: 3). The sins of the children of Israel, and the judgements inflicted upon them, are recorded for our admonition. "Now these things were our examples, to the intent we should not lust after evil things, as they also lusted. * * * Now all these things happened unto them for ensamples: (Gr. by way of figure): and they are written for our admonition" (1 Cor. 10: 6, 11). The Lord Jesus Christ is the promised seed of Abraham, in whom "shall all the nations of the earth be blessed" (Gen. 22: 18). "Now to Abraham and his seed were the promises made. He saith not, and to seeds, as of many; but as of one, and to thy seed, which is Christ" (Gal. 3: 16). Christ was manifested in all their sacrifices, and in their high priest. He was the theme of their prophets, and of their holy Scriptures. Moses and Joshua were types of Him. God sent Moses to deliver His chosen people from Egypt, to teach them His law, and to lead them to the promised land. When Moses was about to leave them, he told them, "The LORD thy God will raise up unto thee a Prophet from the midst of thee, of thy brethren, like unto me; unto Him ye shall hearken." "The LORD said unto me, * * * I will raise them up a Prophet from among their brethren, like unto thee, and will put my words in his mouth; and he shall speak unto them all that I shall command him. And it shall come to pass that whosoever will not hearken unto my words which he shall speak in my name, I will require it of him" (Deut. 18: 15, 18). The Prophet here spoken of is the Lord Jesus Christ. "Philip findeth Nathaniel, and saith unto him, We have found Him of whom Moses in the law, and the prophets, did write, Jesus of Nazareth, the Son of Joseph" (John 1: 45).

Peter, speaking of Christ as the Prophet, said,

"But those things which God before had showed by the mouth of all His prophets, that Christ should suffer, He hath so fulfilled. Repent ye, therefore, and be converted, that your sins may be blotted out, when the times of refreshing shall come from the presence of the Lord. And He shall send Jesus Christ, which before was preached unto you: whom the heaven must receive until the times of restitution of all things, which God hath spoken by the mouth of all His holy prophets since the world began. For Moses truly said unto the fathers, A prophet shall the Lord your God raise up unto you, of your brethren, like unto me; Him shall ye hear in all things whatsoever He shall say unto you" (Acts 3: 18). From heaven God said, "This is my beloved Son: hear Him" (Matt. 17: 5; Mark 9: 7).

As the Prophet, Christ reveals to us the call of God, the word of God, the law of God, the salvation of God, and even the Father Himself. "In the beginning was the Word, and the Word was with God: and the Word was God. * * * And the Word was made flesh, and dwelt among us, and we beheld His glory, the glory of the only begotten of the Father, full of grace and truth. * * * No man hath seen God at any time; the only begotten Son, which is in the bosom of the Father, He hath declared Him" (John 1: 1, 14, 18). "No man knoweth the Son but the Father; neither knoweth any man the Father save the Son, and he to whomsoever the Son will reveal Him" (Matt. 11: 27).

The Jews were in cruel bondage in Egypt without any power to deliver themselves, when God sent Moses to effect their deliverance. In like manner, the chosen children of God are held in slavery by the Devil, the god of this world, helpless and unable to free themselves until Christ delivers them.. The deliverance of the Lord's people is the same in all ages. Five hundred years after Moses, David writes, "O magnify the LORD with me, and let us exalt His name together. I sought the LORD and He heard me, and delivered me from all my fears. They looked unto Him, and were lightened; and their faces were not ashamed. This poor man cried, and the Lord heard him, and saved him out of all his troubles. The angel of the LORD encampeth round about them that fear Him, and delivereth them" (Psm. 34: 3). We read of people crying to Jesus when He was on the earth, and that He heard every cry, and granted every request. "God anointed Jesus of Nazareth with the Holy Ghost and with power; who went about doing good, and healing all that were oppressed of the devil, for God was with Him" (Acts 10: 38). He continues to be, "Jesus Christ the same yesterday, and to-day, and forever" (Heb. 13: 8). "Whosoever shall call upon the name of the Lord shall be saved" (Rom. 10: 13).

As the children of Israel took with them, when they left Egypt, their families, their flocks, and all their substance, so are the children of God required to separate themselves from the world; taking with them their children, and their wealth to be consecrated to God. The Devil, the god of this world, is using the same devices to retain his hold on the children of God, as Pharaoh did to keep the children of Israel in Egypt. When Pharaoh found that he must let them worship God, he proposed that they should remain in Egypt and worship God. "Go ye, sacrifice to your God in the land" (Exod. 8: 25). The Devil suggests, You need not give up the world, you can worship God with the world. Moses said, "It is not meet so to do." And Pharaoh said, "I will let you go, that ye may sacrifice to the Lord, your God, in the wilderness, only ye shall not go very far away" (Exod. 8: 28). The Devil suggests, You need not go so far, you need not separate yourselves from the people of the world in their amusements, their pleasures and their pursuits. You give offence by being over-religious. A good man once said to the writer, I would like to know the dividing line; how near a Christian can live to the world, and yet be a Christian? This he said, not that he wanted to be worldly, but that he would like to avoid giving offence to the worldly. A story is told of a man who wanted a coachman. He asked an applicant for the situation, How near can you drive to a precipice without going over it. I can drive within two feet of it, replied the man. He put the same question to another. He replied, I can drive within one foot. He put the same question to the next; How near can you drive to a precipice without danger of going over it? The man replied, How near? Sure, I would keep as far away from it as I could. He got the place.

Again, Pharaoh was compelled to send for Moses and Aaron; "And he said unto them, Go, serve the Lord, your God; but who are they that shall go? And Moses said, We will go with our young and with our old, with our sons and with our daughters, with our flocks and with our herds will we go; for we must hold a feast unto the Lord. And he said unto them, Let the Lord be so with you, as I will let you go, and your little ones: look to it, for evil is before you. Not so: go now, ye that are men, and serve the Lord; for that ye did desire" (Exod. 10: 8). The Devil makes the same suggestion to many who unite themselves with the people of God, by joining a church, and succeeds in holding them in slavery. They go a little way from Egypt, and leave their children in it. The children must keep up their social standing; they must have amusements, and enjoy themselves; they must mingle with the world; we must shut our eyes in regard to their companions and the kinds of the amusements. They do this even when they know they are demoralizing. They must be educated; and they are sent to Catholic schools, where they are sure to become the followers of Antichrist; and to infidel colleges and infidel theological seminaries, where they will be likely to graduate doubters, or infidels. Many children fail of being saved and are lost, in consequence of the unfaithfulness of their parents, who have been false to the vows they made when joining the Church. Again, when forced to let the people go, Pharaoh made another offer, and said, " Go ye, serve the Lord; only let your flocks and your herds be stayed." * * * "And Moses said, Our cattle also shall go with us; there shall not an hoof be left behind. For thereof must we take to serve the Lord our God" (Exod. 10: 24). Many, who think they are Christians, leave " their flocks in Egypt," their possessions in the world. The result is, where their treasure is their heart is also. Christ says, "Whosoever he be of you that forsaketh not all that he hath, he cannot be my disciple" (Luke 14: 33). You must not only bring yourselves and your flocks out of Egypt, but you must hold them at the disposal of the Lord, or you cannot be His disciples.

When Christ was on the earth, every follower of Him had to forsake father and mother, property, and often give up life itself. And it has been so ever since, in all ages, and in all countries, and especially so in the countries controlled by the Romish and Greek churches: and it is so now everywhere, excepting in the few places where the open Bible and the Spirit of God have made a change. Lot chose Sodom as a residence. The consequence was that he lost every thing, even his influence as a religious man. And he would have perished with Sodom if God had not sent two angels to save him. "And delivered just Lot, vexed with the filthy conversation of the wicked; for that righteous man dwelling among them, in seeing and hearing, vexed his righteous soul from day to day with their unlawful deeds" (2 Pet. 2: 7). "By faith Moses, when he was come to years, refused to be called the son of Pharaoh's daughter; choosing rather to suffer affliction with the people of God, than to enjoy the pleasures of sin for a season; esteeming the reproach of Christ greater riches than the treasures in Egypt: for he had respect unto the recompense of the reward" (Heb. 11: 24). "Wherefore come out from among them, and be ye separate, saith the Lord, and touch not the unclean thing; and I will receive you, and will be a Father unto you, and ye shall be my sons and daughters, saith the Lord Almighty" (2 Cor. 6: 17).

Believer, receive the Lord Jesus Christ as the anointed Prophet of God. Hear Him; obey Him; follow Him; commit yourself entirely to Him. Believing in Him, you will also be anointed with the Holy Spirit. "For all the promises of God in Him are yea, and in Him, Amen, unto the glory of God by us. Now, He which stablisheth us with you in Christ, and hath anointed us, is God; who hath also sealed us, and given the earnest of the Spirit in our hearts" (2 Cor. 1: 20). "That we should be to the praise of His glory, who first trusted in Christ. In whom ye also trusted, after that ye heard the word of truth, the gospel of your salvation: in whom also after that ye believed, ye were sealed with that holy Spirit of promise" (Eph. 1: 12). "Grieve not the holy Spirit of God, whereby ye are sealed" (Eph. 4: 30).

Christ says, "If ye love me, keep my commandments. And I will pray the Father, and He shall give you another Comforter, that He may abide with you forever; even the Spirit of truth; * * * for He dwelleth with you and shall be in you. * * * If a man love me, he will keep my words: and my Father will love him, and we will come unto Him, and make our abode with him" (John 14: 15, 17, 23).

CHRIST, OUR ANOINTED PRIEST.

The High Priest and the priests of the Old Testament were types of Christ and of those who believe in Christ. All believers are now priests. The Lord Jesus Christ is now and forevermore the High Priest. Individual believers in Him are the only priests in His church now. No others are spoken of in the New Testament. They who claim to be successors of the Apostles, to be the "Historical Episcopate," and to be priests, with exclusive powers, have no foundation for their claims in the Scriptures, and should be treated accordingly. Peter writing, "To the strangers scattered through Pontus, Galatia, Cappadocia, Asia and Bithynia, elect according to the foreknowledge of God, through sanctification of the Spirit, unto obedience and sprinkling of the blood of Christ" (1 Peter 1: 1); tells them, "Ye also, as lively stones, are built up a spiritual house, an holy priesthood, to offer up spiritual sacrifices, acceptable to God by Jesus Christ" (1 Pet. 2: 5). "Ye are a chosen generation, a loyal priesthood, an holy nation, a peculiar people, that ye should shew forth the praises of Him who hath called you out of darkness into His marvellous light" (1 Pet. 2: 9). In heaven part of the praise is, "Unto

Him that loved us, and washed us from our sins in His own blood, and hath made us kings and priests unto God and His Father; to Him be glory and dominion for ever and ever. Amen" (Rev. 1: 5). "For thou wast slain, and hast redeemed us to God by Thy blood out of every kindred, and tongue, and nation; and hast made us unto God, kings and priests" (Rev. 5: 9; 20: 6). Through the Lord Jesus Christ, every believer has access to the Father; and whatsoever he asks in His name, it shall be done. The Lord Jesus Christ, the Lamb of God, slain from the foundation of the world, the only sacrifice for sin, is the only High Priest, now and forever. "The Lord sware and will not repent, Thou art a priest forever after the order of Melchisedec. By so much was Jesus made a surety of a better testament. And they truly were many priests, because they were not suffered to continue by reason of death: but He, because He abideth forever, hath His priesthood unchangeable. Wherefore also He is able to save to the uttermost them that draw near unto God through Him, seeing He ever liveth to make intercession for them" (Heb. 7: 21; Rom. 8: 34). He is now the only Mediator between God and man. "For there is one God, and one Mediator between God and men, the man Christ Jesus" (1 Tim. 2: 5). He is our only Advocate with the Father; "If any man sin, we have an advocate with the Father, Jesus Christ the righteous" (1 John 2: 1). Jesus says, "Come unto me, all ye that labour and are heavy-laden, and I will give you rest" (Matt. 11: 28). "Seeing then that we have a great High Priest, that is passed into the heavens, Jesus the Son of God, let us hold fast our profession. For we have not a High Priest which cannot be touched with the feeling of our infirmities; but was in all points tempted like as we are, yet without sin. Let us therefore come boldly unto the throne of grace, that we may obtain mercy, and find grace to help in time of need" (Heb. 4: 14).

The children of God need to be warned against the false priests, who pretend to repeat the sacrifice of Christ by turning a wafer into His body and blood, and then adoring it; a mixture of blasphemy and an idolatry, and an utter perversion of Scripture. Again and again we are told that He offered Himself once only for the sins of His people; and that by that one offering He hath perfected for ever them that are sanctified. "For such a High Priest became us, who is holy, harmless, undefiled, separate from sinners, and made higher than the heavens; who needeth not daily, as those high priests, to offer up sacrifice, first for His own sins, and then for the people's: for this He did once, when He offered up Himself" (Heb. 7: 26). "For Christ is not entered into the holy places made with hands, which are the figures of the true; but into heaven itself, now to appear in the presence of God for us: nor yet that He should offer Himself often, as the High Priest entereth in the holy place every year with the blood of others; for then must He often have suffered since the foundation of the world: but now once in the end of the world hath He appeared to put away sin by the sacrifice of Himself. And as it is appointed unto men once to die, but after this the judgment: so Christ was once offered to bear the sins of many; and unto them that look for Him shall He appear the second time unto salvation" (Heb. 9: 24). "We are sanctified through the offering of the body of Jesus Christ once for all. And every priest standeth daily ministering and offering oftentimes the same sacrifices, which can never take away sins; but this man, after He had offered one sacrifice for sins forever, sat down on the right hand of God; from henceforth expecting till His enemies be made His footstool. For by one offering He hath perfected forever them that are sanctified" (Heb. 10: 10). Believers in the Lord Jesus Christ are warned against the false teachers and the false priests who teach otherwise, and make merchandise of the "souls of men" (Rev. 18: 13). "For the time will come when they will not endure sound doctrine; but after their own lusts shall they heap to themselves teachers, having itching ears; and they shall turn away their ears from the truth, and shall be turned unto fables" (2 Tim. 4: 3). "But there were also false prophets also among the people, even as there shall be false teachers among you, who privily shall bring in damnable heresies, even denying the Lord that bought them, and bring upon themselves swift destruction. And many shall follow their pernicious ways; by reason of whom the way of truth shall be evil spoken of. And through covetousness shall they with feigned words make merchandise of you: whose judgment now of a long time lingereth not, and their damnation slumbereth not" (2 Pet. 2: 1). "By one offering He hath perfected forever them that are sanctified." Their sins are forgiven, and they have now an everlasting life. John 3: 36; 5: 24; 1 John 5: 13. Because they are saved, Paul urges believers, as priests, to offer themselves as a sacrifice. "I beseech you, therefore, brethren, by the mercies of God, that ye present your bodies a living sacrifice, holy, acceptable unto God, which is your reasonable service. (R. V., spiritual worship.) And be not conformed to this world: but be ye transformed by the renewing of your mind, that ye may prove what is that good, and acceptable, and perfect will of God" (Rom. 12: 1).

UNION OF BELIEVERS WITH CHRIST IN HIS DEATH, BURIAL AND RESURRECTION.

THE Lord Jesus Christ is not only our High Priest, but was Himself the sacrifice—the Lamb slain from the foundation of the world. Rev. 13: 8. "For Christ also hath once suffered for sins, the just for the unjust, that He might bring us to God" (1 Pet. 3: 18). "Who His own self bare our sins in His own body on the tree, that we being dead to sins, should live unto righteousness: by whose stripes ye were healed" (1 Pet. 2: 24). "Christ hath redeemed us from the curse of the law, being made a curse for us" (Gal. 3: 13). "Christ our Passover is sacrificed for us" (1 Cor. 5: 7). "He hath borne our griefs, and carried our sorrows" (Isai. 53: 4)). "He was wounded for our transgressions, He was bruised for our iniquities: the chastisement of our peace was upon Him; and with His stripes we are healed" (Isai. 53: 5). That Christ is here spoken of, we see in Matt. 8: 16. "When the even was come, they brought unto Him many that were possessed with devils: and He cast out the spirits with His word, and healed all that were sick: that it might be fulfilled which was spoken by Esaias the prophet, saying, Himself took our infirmities, and bare our sicknesses." Jesus applies to Himself the office of Christ as spoken of Isaiah 61: 1-3. "And there was delivered unto him the book of the prophet Esaias. And when he opened the book, he found the place where it was written, The Spirit of the Lord is upon me, because He hath anointed me to preach the gospel to the poor; He hath sent me to heal the broken-hearted, to preach deliverance to the captives, and recovering of sight to the blind, to set at liberty them that are bruised, to preach the accepted year of the Lord. And he closed the book, and he gave it again to the minister, and sat down. And the eyes of all them that were in the synagogue were fastened on him. And he began to say unto them, This day is this Scripture fulfilled in your ears" (Luke 4: 17). "God was in Christ, reconciling the world unto Himself, not imputing their trespasses unto them. * * * For He hath made Him to be sin for us, who knew no sin; that we might be made the righteousness of God in Him" (2 Cor. 5: 19, 21).

The Scriptures foretold that Christ would come, and would suffer and die in our stead for our sins. "Christ died for us according to the Scriptures" (1 Cor. 15: 3). It was for this purpose that He left the throne of God and came into the world. "Christ Jesus, who being in the form of God, thought it not robbery to be equal with God: but made Himself of no reputation, and took upon Him the form of a servant, and was made in the likeness of men: and being found in fashion as a man, He humbled Himself, and became obedient unto death, even the death of the cross" (Phil. 2: 6). "The Son of man came not to be ministered unto, but to minister, and to give His life a ransom for many" (Matt. 20: 28). The world and all things were created for His coming. Creation and Redemption were to display " The unsearchable riches of Christ; and to make all see what is the fellowship of the mystery, which from the beginning of the world hath been hid in God, who created all things by Jesus Christ: to the intent that now unto the principalities and powers in heavenly places might be known by the church the manifold wisdom of God, according to the eternal purpose which He purposed in Christ Jesus our Lord" (Eph. 3: 8). "Blessed be the God and Father of our Lord Jesus Christ, who hath blessed us with all spiritual blessings in heavenly places in Christ: according as He hath chosen us in Him before the foundation of the world" (Eph. 1: 3). "Forasmuch as ye know that ye were not redeemed with corruptible things, as silver and gold, * * * but with the precious blood of Christ, as of a lamb without blemish and without spot: who verily was foreordained before the foundation of the world" (1 Pet. 1: 18).

Christ offered Himself as a willing sacrifice. Paul writes, "This is a faithful saying, and worthy of all acceptation, that Christ Jesus came into the world to save sinners; of whom I am chief" (1 Tim. 1: 15). Jesus says, "The Son of man is come to seek and to save that which was lost" (Luke 19: 10). He foretold to His disciples the manner of His death. "Jesus said unto them, The Son of man shall be betrayed into the hands of men: aud they shall kill Him, and the third day He shall be raised again" (Matt. 17: 22). "Behold, we go up to Jerusalem; and the Son of man shall be betrayed unto the chief priests and unto the scribes, and they shall condemn Him to death, and shall deliver Him to the Gentiles to mock, and to scourge, and to crucify Him: and the third day He shall rise again" (Matt. 20: 18). It is related, that when Judas came with a band of men and officers from the chief priests and Pharisees to take Him, "Jesus therefore, knowing all things that should come upon Him, went forth, and said unto them, Whom seek ye? They answered Him, Jesus of Nazareth. Jesus saith unto them, I am He" (John 18: 4). He was a willing sacrifice, the Lamb of God, of which all the other sacrifices were types, "For it is not possible that the blood of bulls and of goats should take away sins. Wherefore, when He cometh into the world, He saith, Sacrifice and offering thou wouldest not, but a body hast thou prepared me: in burnt offerings and sacrifices for sin thou hast had no pleasure. Then said I, Lo, I come (in the volume of the book it is written of me) to do Thy will, O God. Above when He said, Sacrifice and offering and burnt offering for sin thou wouldest not, neither hadst pleasure therein; which are offered by the law; then said He, Lo, I come to do Thy will, O God. He taketh away the first, that He may establish the second. By the which will we are sanctified through the offering of the body of Jesus Christ once for all" (Heb. 10: 4, 12).

Through this sacrifice of Christ, believers are counted as having made full atonement for their sins, and are justified in the eye of the law of God. They are also accounted as righteous in the sight of God, Christ having fulfilled the law for them. In the Revelation we read, "After this I beheld, and, lo, a great multitude, which no man could number, of all nations, and kindreds, and people, and tongues, stood before the throne, and before the Lamb, clothed with white robes, and palms in their hands; and cried with a loud voice, saying, Salvation to our God, which sitteth upon the throne, and unto the Lamb" (Rev. 7: 9). In answer to the question, What are these which are arrayed in white robes? "He said unto me, These are they which came out of great tribulation, and have washed their robes, and made them white in the blood of the Lamb" (Rev. 7: 13). The believer is not only counted as righteous, and clothed with Christ's righteousness, but he also receives the gift of righteousness: he receives the spirit of love to God, because he is holy and just, as well as because he is merciful and loving. And the believer is sanctified, and made righteous by the Holy Spirit working in him through the word; according to the prayer of Christ, "Sanctify them through Thy truth: Thy word is truth" (John 17: 17) Paul, speaking of the sacrifices in the Old Testament, says, "For if the blood of bulls and of goats, and the ashes of an heifer, sprinkling the unclean, sanctifieth to the purifying of the flesh: how much more shall the blood of Christ, who through the eternal Spirit offered Himself without spot to God, purge your conscience from dead works to serve the living God" (Heb. 9: 13).

The union of believers with the Lord Jesus Christ in His sufferings, His crucifixion, His death, His burial, His resurrection, His ascension into heaven, and with Him seated on His throne, and as partakers of His glory, is expressly stated in the Scriptures. It is realized in their Christian experience: and it is the great motive for holy living and good works. We are told, "How shall we, that are dead to sin, live any longer therein? Know ye not, that so many of us as were baptized into Jesus Christ were baptized into His death? Therefore we are buried with Him by baptism into death: that like as Christ was raised up from the dead by the glory of the Father, even so we also should walk in newness of life. For if we have been planted together in the likeness of His death, we shall be also in the likeness of His resurrection: knowing this, that our old man is crucified with Him, that the body of sin might be destroyed, that henceforth we should not serve sin. For he that is dead is freed from sin. Now if we be dead with Christ, we believe that we shall also live with Him" (Rom. 6: 2-8). Paul says, "For I through the law am dead to the law, that I might live unto God. I am crucified with Christ: nevertheless I live; yet not I, but Christ liveth in me" (Gal. 2: 19). "Wherefore if ye be dead with Christ from the rudiments of the world, why, as though living in the world, are ye subject to ordinances, (touch not; taste not; handle not; which all are to perish with the using;) after the commandments and doctrines of men?" (Col. 2: 20). "If ye then be risen with Christ, seek those things which are above, where Christ sitteth on the right hand of God. Set your affection on things above, not on things on the earth. For ye are dead, and your life is hid with Christ in God. When Christ, who is our life, shall appear, then shall ye also appear with Him in glory" (Col. 3: 1). "But God, who is rich in mercy; for His great love wherewith He loved us, even when we were dead in sins, hath quickened us together with Christ, (by grace ye are saved;) and hath raised us up together, and made us sit together in heavenly places in Christ Jesus" (Eph. 2: 4). "Who died for us, that whether we wake or sleep, we should live together with Him. Wherefore comfort yourselves together and edify one another, even as also ye do" (1 Thess. 5: 10). "Unto Him that loved us, and washed us from our sins in His own blood, and hath made us kings and priests unto God and His Father; to Him be glory and dominion for ever and ever. Amen" (Rev. 1. 5).

CHRIST, OUR ANOINTED KING.

Anointing was a common practice among the Jews. It was specially used on things and persons consecrated to the service of God. Kings, High Priests, and sometimes prophets, were anointed. The Lord Jesus Christ, who was filled with the Holy Ghost, was thereby consecrated as the Messiah; as prophet, priest, and king. "For He whom God hath sent, speaketh the words of God; for God giveth not the Spirit by measure unto Him" (John 3: 34).

From the beginning of the world a great Deliverer was expected. In the garden of Eden, after the Fall of Eve and Adam, Jehovah God, in putting a curse on the serpent, added, "And I will put enmity between thee and the woman, and between thy seed and her seed; it shall bruise thy head, and thou shalt bruise his heel" (Gen. 3: 15).

From that time there were two distinct races on the earth; the children of God and the children of the Devil. Jesus told the Jews who did not believe in Him, "Ye do the deeds of your father, * * * ye are of your father, the devil" (John 8: 41, 44). In the parable of the sower, Jesus says, "He that soweth the good seed is the son of man; the field is the world; the good seed are the children of the kingdom; but the tares are the children of the wicked one; the enemy that sowed them is the devil" (Matt. 13: 37; Acts 13: 10; 1 John 3: 8, 10, 12).

When Jehovah called Abram to leave his country and kindred, He said unto him, "I will make of thee a great nation * * * and thou shalt be a blessing * * * and in thee shall all families of the earth be blessed" (Gen. 12: 1, 3). Again and again was this promise repeated. "All the nations of the earth shall be blessed in him" (Gen. 18: 18). "In thy seed shall all the nations of the earth be blessed" (Gen. 22: 18; 21: 4; 28: 14). This promise, the Scriptures say, refers to the Lord Jesus Christ. "Ye are the children of the prophets and of the covenant which God made with our fathers, saying unto Abraham, And in thy seed shall all the kindreds of the earth be blessed. Unto you first God, having raised up His Son Jesus, sent Him to bless you, in turning away every one of you from his iniquities" (Acts 3: 25).

"Now, to Abraham and his seed were the promises made. He saith not, And to seeds, as of many; but as one, And to thy seed, which is Christ" (Gal. 3: 16). Nathan was sent to David with the message, "Thus saith Jehovah, * * * I will set up thy seed after thee, * * * and I will stablish the throne of his kingdom for ever, * * *" (2 Sam. 7: 13). The Scripture shows that this promise referred to the Lord Jesus Christ. It was so understood by David, and he wrote accordingly, in a number of the

Psalms, especially in the 2nd, 72nd, and 110th. It was well understood that the Messiah, the Christ, was to be of the seed of David, and that he was the King. The disciples, when threatened by the chief priests and elders, used the very words of the 2nd Psalm, written a thousand years before Christ was born, as part of their prayer to God, and as a promise of Christ. "They lifted up their voice to God with one accord, and said, Lord, Thou art God, which hast made heaven, and earth, and the sea, and all that in them is: who by the mouth of thy servant David, hast said, Why did the heathen rage, and the people imagine vain things? The kings of the earth stood up, and the rulers were gathered together against the Lord, and against His Christ. For of a truth against thy holy child Jesus, whom Thou hast anointed, both Herod and Pontius Pilate, with the Gentiles, and the people of Israel, were gathered together for to do whatsoever Thy hand and Thy counsel determined before to be done" (Acts 4: 26).

In the 72nd Psalm it is written, "All kings shall fall down before Him: all nations shall serve Him. For He shall deliver the needy when he crieth; the poor also, and him that hath no helper. He shall spare the poor and needy, and save the souls of the needy." "His name shall endure for ever; His name shall be continued as long as the sun: and men shall be blessed in Him: all nations shall call Him blessed." In the 110th Psalm, David speaks of the kingdom, the priesthood, the conquest, and the passion of Christ. It commences with, "Jehovah said unto my Lord, sit Thou at my right hand, until I make Thine enemies Thy footstool." Jesus applied this Psalm to Himself. "While the Pharisees were gathered together, Jesus asked them, What think ye of Christ? Whose Son is He? They say unto Him, the Son of David. He saith unto them, How then doth David in spirit call Him Lord, saying, The LORD said unto my Lord, Sit Thou on my right hand till I make Thine enemies Thy footstool? If David then call Him Lord, how is He his son? And no man was able to answer Him a word" (Matt. 22: 41).

The expectation of the coming of the great Messiah king was general in the world when Christ was born. The angel Gabriel told the virgin Mary, speaking of the child, "He shall be great, and shall be called the Son of the Highest: and the Lord God shall give unto Him the throne of His father, David: and He shall reign over the house of Jacob for ever; and of His kingdom there shall be no end" (Luke 1: 32). Pious Jews were praying for, and looking for His coming. We have the account of Simeon, "waiting for the consolation of Israel," and of Anna, "which departed not from the temple, but served God with fastings and prayers night and day. And she coming in that instant gave thanks likewise unto the

Lord, and spoke of Him to all them that looked for redemption in Jerusalem " (Luke :2 25, 37). Angels announced His birth, "Behold, I bring you good tidings of great joy, which shall be to all people. For unto you is born this day in the city of David a Saviour, which is Christ the Lord" (Luke 2: 10). "There came wise men from the east to Jerusalem, saying, Where is He that is born King of the Jews? for we have seen His star in the east and are come to worship Him" (Matt. 2: 1). King Herod was troubled, and demanded of the chief priests and scribes, where Christ should be born? "And they said unto him, in Bethlehem of Judea: for thus it is written by the prophet, And thou, Bethlehem, in the land of Juda, art not the least among the princes of Juda: for out of thee shall come a Governor, that shall rule my people Israel" (Matt. 2: 3). The woman of Samaria, who was living a life of sin, said, " I know that Messias cometh, which is called Christ: when He is come, He will tell us all things " (John 4: 25). " For thus saith Jehovah of hosts, * * * I will shake all nations, and the desire of all nations shall come " (Haggai 2: 7).

Jesus, in many of His parables, illustrated His kingdom. He told Pilate the nature of His kingdom. "Pilate said unto Him, Art Thou the King of the Jews? * * * Jesus answered, My kingdom is not of this world, then would my servants fight that I should not be delivered to the Jews: but now is my kingdom not from hence. Pilate, therefore, said unto Him, Art Thou a king then? Jesus answered, Thou sayest that I am a king. To this end was I born, and for this cause came I into the world" (John 18: 33). When He was about to ascend into heaven He told His disciples, "All power is given unto me in heaven and in earth. Go ye therefore and disciple all nations, baptizing them in the name of the Father, and of the Son, and of the Holy Ghost: teaching them to observe all things whatsoever I have commanded you: and, lo, I am with you alway, even unto the end of the world" (Matt. 28: 18).

"God also hath highly exalted Him, and given Him a name which is above every name: that at the name of Jesus every knee should bow, of things in heaven, and things in earth, and things under the earth; and that every tongue should confess that Jesus Christ is Lord, to the glory of God the Father" (Phil. 2: 9). "God, who at sundry times and in divers manners, spake in time past unto the fathers by the prophets, hath in these last days spoken unto us by His Son, whom He hath appointed heir of all things, by whom also He made the world; who being the brightness of His glory, and the express image of His person, and upholding all things by the word of His power, when He had by Himself purged our sins, sat down on the right hand of the Majesty on high. * * * Unto the Son He saith, Thy throne, O God, is for ever and ever: a sceptre of righteousness is the sceptre of Thy kingdom" (Heb. 1: 1–3, 8).

John says, "And I saw the heaven opened; and behold, a white horse, and He that sat thereon, called Faithful and True; and in righteousness He doth judge and make war. And His eyes are a flame of fire, and upon His head are many diadems; and He hath a name written, which no one knoweth but He Himself. And He is arrayed in a garment sprinkled with blood; and His name is called The Word of God. And the armies which are in heaven followed Him upon white horses, clothed in fine linen, white and pure. And out of His mouth proceedeth a sharp sword; that with it he should smite the nations: and He shall rule them with a rod of iron: and He treadeth the winepress of the fierceness of the wrath of Almighty God. And He hath on His garment and on His thigh a name written, KING OF KINGS AND LORD OF LORDS" (Rev. 19: 11).

A thousand years before Christ came, when all the kingdoms in the world, excepting the kingdom of Israel, were in rebellion against God, David wrote, "All the ends of the world shall remember and turn unto Jehovah; and all the kindreds of the nations shall worship before Thee. For the kingdom is Jehovah's, and He is the governor among the nations" (Psm. 22: 27). Eighteen hundred years have passed since Christ charged His disciples, saying, "All power is given unto me in heaven and in earth. Go ye, therefore, and disciple all nations;" and yet, nearly three quarters of the people in the world have never heard the Gospel. Still the prophecy is sure. His kingdom is progressing fast. The Angel is flying, "having the everlasting Gospel to preach unto them that dwell on the earth, and to every nation, and kindred, and tongue, and people" (Rev. 14: 6). And the other angel is following, "Saying, Babylon is fallen, is fallen, that great city, because she made all nations drink of the wine of the wrath of her fornication" (Rev. 14: 8; 17: 1–18). Rome and popery are falling, but are not yet destroyed, as they surely will be (Rev. 18: 1–24). We shall soon hear the "great voices in heaven, saying, The kingdoms of this world are become the kingdoms of our Lord, and of His Christ; and He shall reign for ever and ever" (Rev. 11: 15).

Child of God! there is no king like your king. Having all power in heaven and in earth; angels, principalities and powers being subject to Him, what can harm you? or injure you? Woe be to any who injure one of the least of His subjects. "Whoso shall offend one of these little ones which believe in me, it were better for him that a millstone were hanged about his neck, and that he were drowned in the depth of the sea" (Matt. 18: 6). Whosoever shall give you a cup of water to drink in my name, because ye belong to Christ, verily I say unto you, he shall not lose his reward" (Mark 10: 41). "Then shall the King say unto them on His right hand, Come, ye blessed of my Father, inherit the kingdom prepared for you from the foundation of the world, * * * Inasmuch as ye have done it unto one of the least of these my brethren, ye have done it unto me" (Matt. 25: 34-40).

As Prophet, Priest, and King, He is able to do everything for His people. "In that He Himself hath suffered being tempted, He is able to succour them that are tempted" (Heb. 2: 18). He "hath an unchangeable priesthood. Wherefore He is able to save them to the uttermost that come unto God by Him, seeing He ever liveth to make intercession for them" (Heb. 7: 24). "Who shall change our vile body, that it may be fashioned like unto His glorious body, according to the working whereby He is able even to subdue all things unto Himself" (Phil. 2: 30). "For I am persuaded, that neither death, nor life, nor angels, nor principalities, nor powers, nor things present, nor things to come, nor height, nor depth, nor any other creature, shall be able to separate us from the love of God, which is in Christ Jesus our Lord" (Rom. 8: 31). "I know whom I have believed, and am persuaded that He is able to keep that which I have committed unto Him against that day" (2 Tim. 1: 12). "It is a faithful saying: for if we be dead with Him, we shall also live with Him: if we suffer, we shall also reign with Him" (2 Tim. 2: 11). "The throne of God and of the Lamb shall be in it; and His servants shall serve Him: and they shall see His face, and His name shall be on their foreheads * * * and they shall reign for ever and ever " (Rev. 22: 3).

UNION WITH CHRIST.—CHRIST OUR LIFE.

The Word of God tells us that the Lord Jesus Christ is the Creator and Sustainer of all life. "He made the worlds," and is "upholding all things by the word of His power" (Heb. 1: 2). "For by Him were all things created, that are in heaven, and that are in earth, visible and invisible, whether they be thrones, or principalities, or powers: all things were created by Him, and for Him: and He is before all things, and by Him all things consist. And He is the head of the body, the Church: who is the beginning, the firstborn from the dead; that in all things He might have the pre-eminence. For it pleased the Father that in Him should all fulness dwell; and having made peace through the blood of His cross, by Him to reconcile all things unto Himself; by Him, I say, whether they be things in earth, or things in heaven" (Col. 1: 16).

The Lord Jesus Christ is also the author, the giver, and the sustainer of spiritual and everlasting life in all the children of God. He quickens them: giving them life, when they were dead in trespasses and sins. "God, who is rich in mercy, for His great love wherewith He loved us, even when we were dead in sins, hath quickened us together with Christ, (by grace ye are saved;) and hath raised us up together, and made us sit together in heavenly places in Christ Jesus. * * * For by grace are ye saved through faith; and that not of yourselves; it is the gift of God: not of works, lest any man should boast. For we are His workmanship, created in Christ Jesus unto good works, which God hath before ordained that we should walk in them" (Eph. 2: 1-10). "God so loved the world, that He gave His only begotten Son, that whosoever believeth in Him should not perish, but have everlasting life" (John 3: 16). "God, who is rich in mercy, for His great love wherewith He loved us, even when we were dead in sins, hath quickened us together with Christ" (Eph. 2: 4). "Christ also hath loved us, and hath given Himself for us an offering and a sacrifice to God" (Eph. 5: 2). "We love Him, because He first loved us" (1 John 4: 19). Christ hath given us life; Christ is our life. Jesus Christ is "The Word, who in the beginning was with God, and who was God. In Him was life; and the life was the light of men" (John 1: 1). "For as the Father raiseth up the dead, and quickeneth them; even so the Son quickeneth whom He will" (John 5: 21). "For as the Father hath life in Himself; so hath He given to the Son to have life in Himself" (John 1: 26). "As Thou hast given Him power over all flesh, that He should give eternal life to as many as Thou hast given Him.

And this is life eternal, that they might know Thee the only living and true God, and Jesus Christ, whom Thou hast sent" (John 17: 2).

Our eternal destiny, everlasting life or everlasting death, depends upon our knowing the Lord Jesus Christ. No wonder that Paul counted all other knowledge as nothing; and said, "I count all things but loss, for the excellency of the knowledge of Christ Jesus my Lord" (Phil. 3: 8). John says, "That which was from the beginning, which we have heard, which we have seen with our eyes, which we have looked upon, and our hands have handled, of the word of life; for the life was manifested, and we have seen it, and bear witness, and shew unto you that eternal life, which was with the Father, and was manifested to us" (1 John 1: 1). "God hath given to us eternal life, and this life is in His Son. He that hath the Son, hath life; and he that hath not the Son of God, hath not life. These things have I written unto you that believe on the name of the Son of God; that ye may know that ye have eternal life" (1 John 5: 11). "For God hath not appointed us to wrath, but to obtain salvation by our Lord Jesus Christ, who died for us, that, whether we wake or sleep, we should live together with Him" (1 Thess. 5: 9).

Jesus said, "I am the way, the truth, and the life: no man cometh unto the Father, but by me" (John 14: 6). "My sheep hear my voice, and I know them, and they follow me: and I give unto them eternal life; and they shall never perish, neither shall any pluck them out of my hand" (John 10: 27). "I am the resurrection, and the life: He that believeth in me, though he were dead, yet shall he live: and whosoever liveth and believeth in me shall never die" (John 11: 25). "Because I live, ye shall live also" (John 14: 19). "He that believeth on the Son hath everlasting life" (John 3: 36). "Hath everlasting life, and shall not come into condemnation; but is passed from death unto life" (John 5: 24). "For ye are dead, and your life is hid with Christ in God. When Christ, who is our life, shall appear, then shall ye also appear with Him in glory" (Col. 3: 3).

Christ is now on the throne of God, having all power in heaven and in earth; therefore, we can say with Paul, "I through the law am dead to the law, that I might live unto God. I am crucified with Christ: nevertheless I live; yet not I, but Christ liveth in me: and the life which I now live in the flesh, I live by the faith of the Son of God, who loved me, and gave Himself for me" (Gal. 2: 19). "For to me to live is Christ, and to die is gain. * * * For I am in a strait betwixt two, having a desire to depart, and to be with Christ; which is far better" (Phil. 1: 21). "We are confident, I say, and willing rather to be absent from the body, and to be present with the Lord" (2 Cor. 5: 8). "But I would not have you to be ignorant, brethren, concerning them which are asleep, that ye sorrow not, even as others which have no hope. For if we believe that Jesus died and rose again, even so them also which sleep in Jesus will God bring with Him" (1 Thess. 1: 13).

UNION WITH CHRIST, CHRIST OUR FOOD.

OF the many types of the new dispensation prefigured in the old, one of the most important and instructive is the Deliverance of the Children of Israel from Egypt, and their journey through the wilderness to the promised land. The whole prefiguring God's deliverance of His people from the slavery of the Devil, the god of this world, and then guiding them, protecting them, and feeding them, until they reach heaven. Salvation, from its beginning to its completion, is entirely of God. What the children of God are to do, is to " Lay aside every weight, and the sin which doth so easily beset us, and let us run with patience the race that is set before us, looking unto Jesus, the author and perfecter of our faith " (Heb. 12: 1).

The chosen of God, born again of the Holy Spirit, delivered from the bondage of the Devil, made temples of the Holy Spirit, are guided by the Spirit, as the children of Israel were led and protected from their enemies by the pillar of cloud and of fire. They are fed with the true Manna, the true Bread from heaven, until they reach there.

The account of the supply of water and of the manna given to the children of Israel is full of instruction. Because of their unbelief, the children of Israel were condemned to journey through a wilderness for a period of forty years; a wilderness in which was neither water nor food.

God supplied them with water by a miracle. He told Moses to speak to a rock and water should issue from it. Instead of speaking to the rock Moses smote it. The water came, but Moses for disobeying God was not allowed to go into the promised land. The Scriptures tell us, "That Rock was Christ." "Moreover, brethren, I would not that ye should be ignorant, how that all our fathers were under the cloud, and all passed through the sea; and were all baptized unto Moses in the cloud and in the sea; and did all eat the same spiritual meat; and did all drink the same spiritual drink; for they drank of that spiritual Rock that followed them: and that Rock was Christ" (1 Cor. 10: 1).

Jesus told the woman of Samaria, "If thou knewest the gift of God, and who it is that saith to thee, Give me to drink, thou wouldest have asked of Him, and He would have given thee living water. * * * Whosoever drinketh of this water shall thirst again: but whosoever drinketh of the water that I shall give him shall never thirst; but the water that I shall give him shall be in him a well of water springing up into everlasting life" (John 4: 10). "In the last day, that great day of the feast, Jesus stood, and cried, saying, If any man thirst, let him come nnto me, and drink. He that believeth on me, as the Scripture hath said, out of his belly shall flow rivers of living water. But this spake He of the Spirit, which they that believe on Him should receive" (John 8: 37).

"The whole congregation of the children of Israel murmured against Moses and Aaron in the wilderness: and the children of Israel said unto them, Would to God we had died by the hand of the Lord in the land of Egypt, when we sat by the flesh pots, and when we did eat bread to the full: for ye have brought us forth into this wilderness, to kill this whole assembly with hunger. Then said the LORD unto Moses, Behold, I will rain bread from heaven for you; and the people shall go out and gather a certain rate every day, that I may prove them, whether they will walk in my law, or no" (Exod. 16: 2). * * * "And when the children of Israel saw it, they said one to another, It is manna: for they wist not what it was. And Moses said unto them, This is the bread which the Lord hath given you to eat. This is the thing which Jehovah hath commandeth, Gather of it every man according to his eating, an omer for every man, according to the number of your persons; take ye every man for them which are in his tent. And the children of Israel did so, and gathered, some more, some less. And when they did mete it with an omer, he that gathered much had nothing over, and he that gathered little had no lack; they gathered every man according to his eating. And Moses said, Let no man leave of it till the morning. Notwithstanding they hearkened not unto Moses; but some of them left of it until the morning, and it bred worms, and stank: and Moses was wroth with them. - And they gathered it every morning, every man according to his eating: and when the sun waxed hot it melted. And it came to pass, that on the sixth day they gathered twice as much bread, two omers for one man: and all the rulers of the congregation came and told Moses. And he said unto them, this is that which the LORD hath said, To-morrow is the rest of the holy sabbath unto the LORD: bake that which ye will bake to-day, and seethe that ye will seethe; and that which remaineth over lay up for you, to be kept until the morning. And they laid it up till the morning as Moses bade: and it did not stink, neither was there any worms therein. And Moses said, Eat that to-day, for to-day is a sabbath unto the Lord: to-day ye shall not find it in the field. Six days ye shall gather it, but on the seventh day, which is the sabbath, in it there shall be none. And it came to pass, that there went out some of the people on the seventh day for to gather, and they found none " (Ex. 16: 2). "And the children of Israel did eat manna forty years, until they came to land inhabited; they did eat manna, until they came unto the borders of the land of Canaan " (Exod. 16: 35).

After Jesus had fed the five thousand met with five barley loaves and two small fishes, which a lad had; and after they were filled and twelve baskets full were left, the men said "This is of a truth that prophet that should come into the world. When Jesus, therefore, perceived that they would come and take Him by force to make Him a king, He departed again into a mountain Himself alone" (John 6: 9). The following day the people sought Him. Jesus said to them, "Verily, verily, I say unto you, Ye seek me, not because ye saw the miracles, but because ye did eat of the loaves, and were filled. Labour not for the meat which perisheth, but for that meat which endureth unto everlasting life, which the Son of man shall give unto you: for Him hath God the Father sealed. Then said they unto Him, What shall we do, that we might work the works of God? Jesus answered and said unto them, This is the work of God, that ye believe on Him whom He hath sent. They said, therefore, unto Him, What sign shewest thou then, that we may see, and believe thee? What dost thou work? Our fathers did eat manna in the desert; as it is written, He gave them bread from heaven to eat. Then Jesus said unto them, Verily, verily, I say unto you, Moses gave you not that bread from heaven; but my Father giveth the true bread from heaven. For the bread of God is He which cometh down from heaven, and giveth life unto the world. Then said they unto Him, Lord, evermore give us this bread. And Jesus said unto them, I am the bread of life: he that cometh to me shall never hunger; and he that believeth on me shall never thirst. * * * Verily, verily, I say unto you, he that believeth on me hath everlasting life. I am that bread of life. Your fathers did eat manna in the wilderness, and are dead. This is the bread which cometh down from heaven, that a man may eat thereof, and not die. I am the living bread which came down from heaven: if any man eat of this bread, he shall live forever: and the bread that I will give is my flesh, which I give for the life of the world. * * * It is the Spirit that quickeneth; the flesh profiteth nothing: the words that I speak unto you, they are spirit, and they are life" (John 6: 26, 47, 63).

In all ages the Word of God was to be fed upon as spiritual food. "Moreover he said unto me, Son of man, all my words that I shall speak unto thee receive in thine heart, and hear with thine ears" (Ezek 3: 10). The Lord spake to Ezekiel, "Open thy mouth, and eat that I give thee. And when I looked, behold, a hand was sent unto me; and, lo, a roll of a book was therein; and he spread it before me; and it was written within and without: and there was written therein lamentations, and mourning, and woe. Moreover he said unto me, Son of man, eat that thou findest; eat this roll, and go speak unto the house of Israel" (Ezek. 2: 8; 3: 1). Those sent to call sinners to repentance must eat the book, the Bible, the word of God, even if it contains "written therein lamentations, and mourning, and woe." They must deliver that word, "and tell them, Thus saith the Lord God; whether they will hear or whether they will forbear." Ezekiel was told to do this, even after he was told, "But the house of Israel will not hearken unto thee; for they will not hearken unto me" (Ezek. 2). He must first, "Eat the book," and then deliver the message contained in it, even when told they would not hear him. John writes, "I saw another mighty angel,": * * * " and he had in his hand a little book " * * * " and the voice which I heard from heaven spoke unto me again, and said, Go and take the little book which is open in the hand of the angel:" * * * "And I went unto the angel, and said unto him, Give me the little book. And he said unto me, Take it and eat it up." * * * "And I took the little book out of the angel's hand, and ate it up." * * * "And he said unto me, Thou must prophesy again before many peoples, and nations, and tongues, and kings" (Rev. 10: 1). We must eat Christ, as He is revealed in His word; that we may have everlasting life and be enabled to carry the message of God to others. The whole Bible is the presentation of Christ; He is the Word. "In the beginning was the Word, and the Word was with God, and the Word was

God." * * * "And the Word was made flesh, and dwelt among us" (John 1: 1, 14).

We make a great mistake in not studying the Old Testament and "eating" it. It was the only Scriptures in the time of Christ and of the apostles. Christ constantly referred to them to prove that He was the Christ; that Christ was to suffer; "beginning at Moses and all the prophets, He expounded unto them in all the Scriptures the things concerning Himself," and said unto them, "All things must be fulfilled, which were written in the law of Moses, and in the prophets, and in the psalms concerning me" (Luke 24: 27, 44). "Ye do err not knowing the Scriptures" (Matt. 22: 29). "They are they which testify of me" (John 5: 39). It was to the Old Testament that Paul referred when he wrote to Timothy, "From a child thou hast known the Holy Scriptures, which are able to make thee wise unto salvation through faith which is in Christ Jesus. All Scripture is given by inspiration of God, and is profitable for doctrine, for reproof, for correction, for instruction in righteousness: that the man of God may be perfect, thoroughly furnished unto all good works" (2 Tim. 3: 15).

Therefore, we are to see the Lord Jesus Christ in all the Holy Scriptures; from the promise of Him made to Adam, and Abel's sacrifice of the lamb in Genesis, to the "Lamb as it had been slain, in the midst of the throne," in Revelation. We are to receive that Word, feed upon that Word, believe that Word, and thus grow in grace and in the knowledge of our Lord and Saviour Jesus Christ. "Till we all come in the unity of the faith, and of the knowledge of the Son of God, unto a perfect man, unto the measure of the stature of the fulness of Christ" (Eph. 4: 13).

Beware of any suggestion of the Devil, whether coming to you directly, or through others, causing you to doubt that Word. Beware of false priests putting the traditions of their church in the place of that Word. Beware of the assertions of some pretending to a higher criticism. "Keep that which is committed to thy trust, avoiding profane and vain babblings, and oppositions of science falsely so called, which some professing have erred concerning the faith" (1 Tim. 6: 20).

Beware of adding to, or taking from the Scriptures. "Ye shall not add to the word which I command you, neither shall ye diminish ought from it" (Deut. 4: 2). "What thing soever I command you, observe to do it: thou shalt not add thereto, nor diminish from it" (Deut. 12: 32). "If any man shall add unto these things, God shall add unto him the plagues that are written in this book: and if any man shall take away from the words of the book of this prophecy, God shall take away his part out of the book of life" (Rev. 22: 18). "As we said before, so say I now again, If any man preach any other gospel unto you than that ye have received, let him be accursed" (Gal. 1: 8).

"As new-born babes, desire the sincere milk of the Word, that ye may grow thereby" (1 Pet. 2: 2). Christ is the true food of the soul. The soul needs spiritual food. Christ's word, and Christ's broken body, and Christ's blood shed for us, as revealed in that Word, when received into the soul by faith, nourish and strengthen us. As the faith of the Jew was strengthened every time he partook of the feast commemorating the Passover, so is the faith of the Christian increased in the sacrifice of the Lord Jesus Christ for us, every time, that with faith in that sacrifice, he partakes of the feast instituted by the Lord Jesus Christ, as a commemoration of it. "For as often as ye eat this bread, and drink this cup, ye do shew the Lord's death till He come" (1 Cor. 11: 26).

In feeding upon Christ, as He is revealed in His word, we are to look to the Holy Ghost promised to His disciples. "He shall teach you all things, and bring all things to your remembrance, whatsoever I have said unto you" (John 14: 26). "He will guide you into all truth:" "He shall glorify me: for He shall receive of mine, and shall shew it unto you. All things that the Father hath are mine: therefore said I, that He shall take of mine, and shall shew it unto you" (John 16: 13). Doing this, our souls will grow in the knowledge of

God and of Christ. "And this is life eternal, that they might know Thee the only true God, and Jesus Christ, whom Thou hast sent" (John 17: 3).

There is this difference between the manna and Christ. He said to the Jews, "Verily, verily, I say unto you, He that believeth on me hath everlasting life. I am that bread of life. Your fathers did eat manna in the wilderness, and are dead. This is the bread which cometh down from heaven, that a man may eat thereof, and not die. I am the living bread which came down from heaven: if any man eat of this bread he shall live for ever" (John 6: 47). As it was with the manna, the Lord Jesus Christ is the only spiritual food provided for the children of God for their whole journey through this world. There is an abundant supply for them all. It has been continued from the beginning, and will continue until the end of the world. It is suited for all the generations of men; for all nations; for all ages, old and young; for all classes; king or beggar, rich and poor, learned and ignorant. All must gather it daily; all must receive it; all must assimilate it, and live upon it, or they will starve and die. They must also gather it for their household.

To enable us to realize more fully the great things which accompany salvation, and the great privileges we enjoy as children of God, we are urged to "grow in the grace and knowledge of our Lord and Saviour Jesus Christ" (2

Pet. 3: 18). Peter begins his second epistle addressed "to them that have obtained a like precious faith with us in the righteousness of our God and Saviour Jesus Christ: grace to you and peace be multiplied in the knowledge of God and of Jesus our Lord: seeing that His divine power hath granted unto us all things that pertain unto life and godliness, through the knowledge of Him that called us by His own glory and virtue; whereby He hath granted unto us His precious and exceeding great promises; that by these ye may become partakers of the divine nature" (2 Pet. 1: 2). The "all things" come through knowledge of Christ. This knowledge and these "precious and exceeding great promises" are contained in His word. Studying that word, believing that word, the child of God receives this knowledge, and those promises; and becomes a "partaker of the divine nature."

We are told to pray, "Give us this day our daily bread." We must bear in mind, in using this prayer, that the true Bread given to us by God, is the Lord Jesus Christ. We need a fresh supply of bread every day. It must be eaten and assimilated by us, and become a part of us, or it will do us no good. Looking to Christ, now and then, as an example, or reading about Him, or hearing about Him occasionally, is not enough. We must receive Him as our food, and He must become our life, and live in us, day by day, until we reach heaven. Paul said,

"I live, yet not I, but Christ liveth in me" (Gal. 2: 20). By His death Jesus became the Bread of life. He said, "Verily, verily, I say unto you, Except a corn of wheat fall into the ground and die, it abideth alone: but if it die, it bringeth forth much fruit. * * * And I, if I be lifted up from the earth, will draw all men unto me. This He said, signifying what death He should die" (John 12: 24, 32). In Him is everything we need to sustain the life which He has given to us. We have His word: all we have to do is to gather it and feed upon it. We need to grow in grace and in the knowledge of Him. "As new-born babes, desire the sincere milk of the word, that ye may grow thereby" (1 Pet. 2: 2). We need light, and guidance, and understanding. "The entrance of Thy words giveth light; it giveth understanding to the simple" (Psm. 119: 130). "Thy word is a lamp unto my feet, and a light unto my path" (Psm. 119: 105). We need quickening. "My soul cleaveth unto the dust: quicken Thou me according to Thy word" (Psm. 119: 25, 50). We need sanctification. "Sanctify them through Thy truth, Thy word is truth" (John 17: 17). We need wisdom and righteousness. "But of Him are ye in Christ Jesus, who of God is made unto us wisdom, and righteousness, and sanctification, and redemption" (1 Cor. 1: 30). "For Christ is the end of the law for righteousness to every one that believeth" (Rom. 10: 4). We are to "receive with meekness the engrafted word, which is able to save your souls" (James 1: 21). "The word of His grace, which is able to build you up, and to give you an inheritance among all them that are sanctified" (Acts 20: 32). We need peace and comfort. Jesus says, "Peace I leave with you, my peace I give unto you: not as the world giveth, give I unto you. Let not your heart be troubled, neither let it be afraid" (John 14: 27). "Leave thy fatherless children, I will preserve them alive; and let thy widows trust in me" (Jer. 49: 11). In Christ we have life. "He that heareth my word and believeth on Him that sent me hath everlasting life, and shall not come into condemnation; but is passed from death unto life" (John 5: 24). "Whosoever liveth, and believeth in me, shall never die" (John 11: 26). "Because I live, ye shall live also" (John 14: 19). We need strength. "He said unto me, My grace is sufficient for thee: for my strength is made perfect in weakness" (2 Cor. 12: 9). We have a desire to do good works. Christ says, "Abide in me, and I in you. As the branch cannot bear fruit of itself, except it abide in the vine; no more can ye, except ye abide in me. I am the vine, ye are the branches: He that abideth in me, and I in Him, the same bringeth forth much fruit: for without me ye can do nothing" (John 15). Paul says, "I can do all things through Christ which strengtheneth me" (Phil. 4: 13). The believer in Christ can appropriate all the promises in the Bible. "All the promises of God in

Him are yea, and in Him Amen, unto the glory of God by us" (2 Cor. 1: 20). "We know that all things work together for good to them that love God" (Rom. 8: 28). "For I am persuaded that neither death, nor life, nor angels, nor principalities, nor powers, nor things present, nor things to come, nor height, nor depth, nor any other creature, shall be able to separate us from the love of God, which is in Christ Jesus our Lord" (Rom. 8: 38). "All things are yours; whether Paul, or Apollos, or Cephas, or the world, or life, or death, or things present, or things to come; all are yours; and ye are Christ's; and Christ is God's" (1 Cor. 3: 21). Believing these words of Christ, we receive Him; are united to Him; we grow in grace and in knowledge of Him; and have everlasting life. Christ is the true Bread from heaven given by God.

UNION WITH CHRIST.

FATHER—BROTHER—FRIEND.

Among the many names by which the Lord Jesus Christ reveals Himself to us, showing the close and intimate union there is between Him and believers in Him, is that of Father. Although Christ is spoken of as the Son of the Father, yet the Scriptures speak of Christ also as Father; as one with the Father, and as having a special seed; those believing in Him. "For unto us a child is born, unto us a son is given, and the government shall be upon His shoulder: and His name shall be called Wonderful, Counsellor, Mighty God, Everlasting Father, Prince of Peace. Of the increase of His Government and of peace there shall be no end" (Isai. 9: 6). Jesus said, "I snd my Father are one" (John 10: 30). The Scriptures tell us that by the Lord Jesus Christ "were all things created that are in heaven, and that are in earth, visible and invisible, whether they be thrones, or dominions, or principalities, or powers: all things were created by Him and for Him, and He is before all things, and by Him all things consist. And He is the head of the body, the Church" (Col. 1: 16). John, speaking of Jesus, says, "He was in the world, and the world was made by Him, and the world knew Him not" (John 1: 10). "God, who at sundry times and in divers manners, spake in time past unto the fathers by the prophets, hath in these latter days spoken unto us by His Son, whom He hath appointed heir of all things, by whom also He made the world; who being the brightness of His glory, and the express image of His person, and upholding all things by the word of His power, when He had by Himself purged our sins, sat down on the right hand of the Majesty on high" (Heb. 1: 1). As the Creator and upholder of all things, the Lord Jesus Christ may well be named "The Mighty God, Everlasting Father." He is also the Father of them who believe in Him, they are His spiritual seed. "When thou shalt make his soul an offering for sin, he shall see his seed, he shall prolong his days, and the pleasure of Jehovah shall prosper in his hand. He shall see of the travail of his soul, and shall be satisfied" (Isai. 53: 10). "A seed shall serve Him, it shall be accounted to the Lord for a generation" (Psm. 22· 30). He says, "For both He that sanctified and they who are sanctified are all of one. * * * "Behold I and the children which God hath given me" (Heb. 2: 11, 13).

BROTHER.

Jesus calls His disciples, Brethren: " For it became Him, for whom are all things, and by whom are all things, in bringing many sons unto glory, to make the author of their saltion perfect through sufferings. For both He that sanctifieth and they who are sanctified are all of one: for which cause He is not ashamed to call them brethren, saying, I will declare thy name unto my brethren" (Heb. 2: 10). His relationship to believers is far closer than any earthly relationship. When He was told that His mother and His brethren were without, desiring to see Him, "He stretched forth His hand toward His disciples and said, Behold my mother and my brethren! For whosoever shall do the will of my Father which is in heaven, the same is my brother, and sister, and mother" (Matt. 12: 49). After His resurrection, Jesus met the women who were sent by the angel to tell His disciples that He was risen, and said unto them, "Be not afraid: go tell my brethren that they go into Galilee, and there shall they see me" (Matt. 28: 9). When He revealed Himself to Mary Magdalen, "Jesus saith unto her, Cling not to me (Take not hold on me); for I am not yet ascended to my Father: but go to my brethren, and say unto them, I ascend unto my Father, and your Father; and to my God, and your God" (John 20: 17). When Christ is on His throne judging the world, His disciples will be acknowledged before the universe. "Come, ye blessed of my Father, inherit the kingdom prepared for you from the foundation of the world." Then any act of kindness done to a disciple will be acknowledged as done unto Him. "And the King shall answer and say unto them, Verily, I say unto you, Inasmuch as ye have done it unto one of the least of these my brethren, ye have done it unto me" (Matt. 25: 40). The children of God were predestinated to be brethren of Christ. "For whom He did foreknow, He also did predestinate to be conformed to the image of His Son, that he might be the first born among many brethren" (Rom. 8: 29). Believers in the Lord Jesus Christ, "The Spirit itself beareth witness with our spirit, that we are the children of God: and if children, then heirs; heirs of God, and joint-heirs with Christ" (Rom. 8: 16), our elder Brother.

FRIEND.

Jesus also honors His disciples by making them His friends. A friend is one whom we love and esteem above others; to whom we impart our minds more familiarly than to others; and that from a confidence of his integrity and good will towards us; thus Jonathan and David were mutually friends. The Scriptures say, "A friend loveth at all times" (Prov. 17: 17). "There is a friend that sticketh closer than a brother" (Prov. 18: 24). "Faithful are the wounds of a friend" (Prov. 27: 6). "Ointment and perfume rejoice the heart; so doth the sweetness of a man's friend by hearty counsel" (Prov. 27: 9). "Jehovah spoke unto Moses face to face, as a man speaketh unto his friend" (Exod. 33: 11). In the Bible Abraham is often called the "Friend of God." "And the Lord said, Shall I hide from Abraham that thing which I do; seeing that Abraham shall surely become a great and mighty nation, and all the nations of the earth shall be blessed in him?" (Gen. 18: 17) "And the Scripture was fulfilled which saith, Abraham believed God, and it was imputed unto him for righteousness: and he was called the Friend of God" (James 2: 23; Exod. 33: 11; 2 Chron. 20: 7; Isai. 41: 8). Jesus said, "Greater love hath no man than this, that a man lay down his life for his friend. Ye are my friends, if ye do whatsoever I command you. Henceforth I call ye not servants; for the servant knoweth not what his lord doeth: but I have called you friends; for all things that I have heard of my Father I have made known unto you" (John 15: 13). This was said, "When Jesus knew that His hour was come that He should depart out of this world unto the Father," and "knowing that the Father had given all things into His hands, and that He was come from God, and went to God" (John 13: 1, 3). As He was about to ascend to the throne of the universe, He assures His disciples that He is their Friend. Child of God! our Father, Brother, Friend, has all power in heaven and earth.

UNION WITH CHRIST.

HUSBAND AND WIFE.

The union between Christ and His Church is described in the Scriptures by words which are used for the closest, the most intimate, the most confiding and most loving of all human relationships: that of husband and wife. This relationship is frequently spoken of in the Old Testament, as well as the New: "For thy Maker is thine husband: Jehovah of hosts is His name; and thy Redeemer the Holy One of Israel; the God of the whole earth shall He be called" (Isai. 54: 5). "As the bridegroom rejoiceth over the bride, so shall thy God rejoice over thee" (Isai. 62: 5). "Turn, O backsliding children, saith Jehovah; for I am married unto you" (Jer. 3: 14; 31: 32). "Son of Man, cause Jerusalem to know her abominations, and say, Thus saith the Lord God unto Jerusalem; Thy birth and thy nativity is of the land of Canaan; thy father was an Amorite, and thy mother a Hittite. * * * Thou wast cast out in the open field. * * * And when I passed by thee, and saw thee polluted in thine own blood, I said unto thee when thou wast in thy blood, Live; yea, I said unto thee when thou wast in thy blood, Live. I have caused thee to multiply as the bud of the field, and thou hast increased and waxen great. * * * I thoroughly washed away thy blood from thee, and I anointed thee with oil. I clothed thee also with ornaments, and I put bracelets upon thy hands, and a chain on thy neck. And I put a jewel on thy forehead, and ear-rings in thine ears, and a beautiful crown upon thine head. Thus wast thou decked with gold and silver; and thy raiment was of fine linen, and silk, and broidered work; thou didst eat fine flour, and honey, and oil; and thou wast exceeding beautiful, and thou didst prosper into a kingdom. And thy renown went forth among the heathen for thy beauty: for it was perfect through my comeliness, which I had put upon thee, saith the Lord God. But thou didst trust in thine own beauty, and playedst the harlot. * * * I will judge thee, as women that break wedlock and shed blood are judged. * * * And I will cause thee to cease from playing the harlot. * * * So will I make my fury toward thee to rest, and my jealousy shall depart from thee. * * * Nevertheless, I will remember my covenant with thee in the days of thy youth, and I will establish unto thee an everlasting covenant" (Ezek. 16). "And I will betroth thee unto me forever; yea, I will betroth thee unto me in righteousness, and in judgment, and in loving-kindness, and in mercies. I will even betroth thee unto me in faithfulness: and thou shalt know Jehovah" (Hosea 2: 19). Paul writes, "I am jealous over you with a godly jealousy: for I have espoused you to one husband, that I may present you as a chaste virgin to Christ. But I fear, lest by any means, as the serpent beguiled Eve, through his subtilty, so your minds should be corrupted from the simplicity that is in Christ" (2 Cor. 11: 2). "Wives, submit yourselves unto your own husbands, as unto the Lord. For the husband is the head of the wife, even as Christ is the head of the Church: and He is the Saviour of the body. Therefore as the Church is subject unto Christ, so let the wives be to their own husbands in everything. Husbands, love your wives, even as Christ also loved the Church, and gave Himself for it; that He might sanctify and cleanse it with the washing of water by the word, that He might present it to Himself a glorious Church, not having spot, or wrinkle, or any such thing; but that it should be holy and without blemish" (Eph. 5: 22).

The Church is called the wife of the Lamb in the Revelation. "Let us be glad and rejoice, and give honour to Him: for the marriage of the Lamb is come, and His wife hath made herself ready. And to her was granted that she should be arrayed in fine linen, clean and white: for the fine linen is the righteousness of saints" (Rev. 19: 7). "For the fine linen is the righteous acts of the saints" (Rev. 19: 8, Revised Version). The saints are not only clothed with the righteousness of Christ, but they are also adorned with the graces produced in them by the Holy

Spirit. "The fruit of the Spirit is love, joy peace, long suffering, kindness, goodness, faithfulness, meekness, temperance" (Gal. 5: 22). "Whose adorning let it not be the outward adorning, * * * but let it be the hidden man of the heart in the incorruptible apparel of a meek and quiet spirit, which is in the sight of God of great price" (1 Pet. 3: 3). "I desire therefore that the men pray in every place, lifting up holy hands, without wrath and disputing. In like manner, that women adorn themselves * * * through good works" (1 Tim. 2: 8). "I will greatly rejoice in the LORD, my soul shall be joyful in my God: for He hath clothed me with the garments of salvation, He hath covered me with the robe of righteousness, as a bridegroom decketh himself with ornaments, and as a bride adorneth herself with her jewels" (Isai. 61: 10).

"And I saw a new heaven and a new earth: for the first heaven and the first earth were passed away; and there was no more sea. And I John saw the holy city, New Jerusalem, coming down from God out of heaven, prepared as a bride adorned for her husband. And I heard a great voice out of heaven saying, Behold, the tabernacle of God is with men, and He will dwell with them, and they shall be His people, and God Himself shall be with them, and be their God. And God shall wipe away all tears from their eyes; and there shall be no more death, neither sorrow, nor crying, neither shall there be any more pain: for the former things are passed away" (Rev. 21: 1).

The marriage of Christ and His Church is typified by that of husband and wife. As in a true marriage there must be mutual consent and love, mutual esteem and confidence, mutual surrender and consecration, which can only be founded on knowledge of each other; so, in a far greater degree is all this between Christ and His Bride, the Church. Being both partakers of one Spirit, their union is a spiritual union Christ loved the Church, and gave Himself for it" (Eph. 5: 25). The believer gives up all things for Christ. Christ says, "He that loveth father or mother more than me, is not worthy of me: and he that loveth son or daughter more than me, is not worthy of me; and he that taketh not his cross and followeth after me, is not worthy of me" (Matt. 10: 37). "Every one that hath forsaken houses or brethren, or sisters, or father, or mother, or wife, or children, or lands, for my name's sake, shall receive an hundred-fold, and shall inherit everlasting life" (Matt. 19: 29).

The Bible uses very strong language to members of the church who cling to the world. "Ye adulterers and adulteresses, know ye not that the friendship of the world is enmity with God? whosoever, therefore, will be a friend of the world, is the enemy of God" (James 4: 4).

The Bride is called to suffer with Christ in this world; but believers are told, "Rejoice, inasmuch as ye are partakers of Christ's sufferings; that when His glory shall be revealed, ye may be glad also with exceeding joy" (1 Pet. 4: 13). "It is a faithful saying: For if we be dead with Him, we shall also live with Him: if we suffer, we shall also reign with Him" (2 Tim. 2: 11).

Christ spoke of the coming marriage feast in the parable of the King, who made a marriage feast for his son (Matt. 22: 2); and in the parable of the Ten Virgins, who went forth to meet the Bridegroom (Matt. 25: 1). In Revelation we have accounts of the glorious mansion prepared by Christ for His Bride, His Church, (Rev. 21: 1) and also, of the festivities of the marriage feast. "Let us be glad and rejoice, and give honor to Him: for the marriage of the Lamb is come, and His wife hath made herself ready" (Rev. 19: 7). "And He said unto me, Write, Blessed are they which are called unto the marriage supper of the Lamb" (Rev. 19: 9). The husband and wife "shall be no more twain. Wherefore they are no more twain, but one flesh" (Matt. 19; 5; Mark 10; 8). "But he that is joined unto the Lord is one spirit" (1 Cor. 6: 17). "For we are members of His body, of His flesh, and of His bones" (Eph. 5: 30).

Partakers of one Spirit, believers are one with Christ. Praying for them, Christ said, "They are not of the world, even as I am not of the world * * * sanctify them through Thy truth; Thy word is truth. * * * That they all may be one; as Thou, Father, art in me, and I in thee, that they also may be one in us * * * I in them, and Thou in me" (John 17: 16, 21).

CHRIST THE CORNER-STONE.

BELIEVERS LIVING STONES BUILT ON HIM.

CHRIST and His Church are represented in the Scriptures as being united, as a holy temple in the Lord. His people are said to be built up on Him as living stones on a living corner-stone—the living corner-stone giving support and strength to the whole building; uniting each stone with Him, and with one another, by one Spirit and one life.

Christ is the Foundation of all of our knowledge of God. "No man knoweth the Son, but the Father; neither knoweth any man the Father, save the Son, and he to whomsoever the Son will reveal Him" (Matt. 11: 27; Luke 10: 22). "No man hath seen God at any time; the only begotten Son, which is in the bosom of the Father, He hath declared Him" (John 1: 18).

Jesus said, "I am the way, the truth, and the life; no man cometh unto the Father, but by me. If ye had known me, ye should have known my Father also: and from henceforth ye know Him, and have seen Him." "He that hath seen me hath seen the Father" (John 14: 6, 9).

Christ is the Foundation of the Holy Scriptures. He is the word. "In the beginning was the Word, and the Word was with God, and the Word was God." "And the Word was made flesh, and dwelt among us" (John 1: 1, 14). The whole Bible, from beginning to the end, is founded on Christ; reveals Christ; and is Christ.

Christ is the Foundation of the Church. "For other foundation can no man lay than that is laid, which is Jesus Christ." "Know ye not that ye are the temple of God, and that the Spirit of God dwelleth in you? If any man defile the temple of God, him shall God destroy; for the temple of God is holy, which temple ye are" (1 Cor. 3: 11, 16).

Seven hundred years before Christ came, Isaiah wrote, "Therefore, thus saith the Lord God, Behold, I lay in Zion for a foundation a stone, a tried stone, a precious corner-stone, a sure foundation: he that believeth shall not make haste" (Isai. 28: 16). Peter, quoting this, says, "Wherefore also it is contained in the Scripture, Behold, I lay in Sion a chief corner-stone, elect, precious; and he that believeth on Him shall not be confounded. Unto you, therefore, which believe He is precious: but unto them which be disobedient, the stone which the builders disallowed, the same is made the head of the corner, and a stone of stumbling, and a rock of offence, even to them which stumble at the Word, being disobedient: whereunto also they were appointed. But ye are a chosen generation, a royal priesthood, a holy nation, a peculiar people; that ye should shew forth the praises of Him who hath called you out of darkness into His marvellous light" (1 Pet. 2: 6). Before this he writes, "But the word of the Lord endureth forever. And this is the Word which, by the Gospel, is preached unto you. Wherefore, laying aside all malice, and all guile, and hypocrisies, and envies, and all evil speakings, as new-born babes, desire the sincere milk of the Word, that ye may grow thereby; if so be ye have tasted that the Lord is gracious. To whom coming, as unto a living stone, disallowed indeed of men, but chosen of God, and precious, ye also, as lively stones, are built up a spiritual house, a holy priesthood, to offer up spiritual sacrifices, acceptable to God by Jesus Christ" (1 Pet. 1: 25; 2: 1).

Christ is the corner-stone on which all believers are built as living stones. "For through Him we both have access by one Spirit unto the Father." "And are built upon the foundation of the apostles and prophets, Jesus Christ Himself being the chief corner-stone; in whom all the building fitly framed together groweth unto a holy temple in the Lord: in whom ye also are builded together for a habitation of God through the Spirit" (Eph. 2: 18, 20). "Rooted and built up in Him, and stablished in the faith, as ye have been taught, abounding therein with thanksgiving. Beware lest any man spoil you through philosophy and vain deceit, after the tradition of men, after the rudiments of the world, and not after Christ. For in Him dwelleth all the fulness of the Godhead bodily. And ye are complete in Him, who is the head of all principality and power" (Col. 2: 7). "But let every man take heed how he buildeth thereupon. For other foundation can no man lay than that is laid, which is Jesus Christ" (1 Cor. 3: 10).

CHRIST AND BELIEVERS—SHEPHERD AND SHEEP.

In many parts of the Holy Scriptures, the Old Testament and the New, the children of God are called sheep; and Jehovah, the Lord Jesus Christ, is called their Shepherd. These passages are full of important religious truth, and Christian experience. A sheep is the most helpless and defenceless of all animals: is liable to go astray; is unable to find its way back; and needs the constant watchful care of the shepherd to guard it, feed it, guide it, and to fetch it back when astray. Such is the case with every child of God: and he may well rejoice that Jehovah, the Lord Jesus Christ, is his Shepherd.

As a sheep, the believer has heard the call of Christ. "He calleth His own sheep by name, and leadeth them out." He knows each one of His sheep individually by name. "And they follow Him: for they know His voice" (John 10: 3). He has called them out of Egypt, the world; and delivered them from Satan, the god of this world. He will lead them through the wilderness, feed them with the heavenly manna, and carry them safely to the promised land. "When the Son of man shall come in His glory, and all the holy angels with Him, then shall He sit upon the throne of His glory: and before Him shall be gathered all nations: and He shall separate them one from another as a shepherd divideth his sheep from the goats: and He shall set the sheep on his right hand, but the goats on the left. Then shall the King say unto them on His right hand, Come, ye blessed of my Father, inherit the kingdom prepared for you from the foundation of the world" (Matt. 25: 31).

God "smote all the firstborn in Egypt; the chief of their strength in the tabernacles of Ham: but made His own people to go forth like sheep, and guided them in the wilderness like a flock" (Psm. 78: 51). "So we Thy people and sheep of Thy pasture will give Thee thanks forever: we will show forth Thy praise to all generations" (Psm. 79: 73). "For He is our God; and we are the people of His pasture, and the sheep of His hand" (Psm. 95: 7; 100: 3). The experience of the sheep is the same in all ages. The Psalmist writes, "I have gone astray like a lost sheep" (Psm. 119: 176). Isaiah writes, "All we like sheep have gone astray; we have turned every one to his own way; and the Lord hath laid on Him the iniquity of us all" (Isai. 53: 6). Peter writes, "For ye were as sheep going astray; but are now returned unto the Shepherd and Bishop of your souls" (1 Pet. 2: 25). Before Christ came, the children of Israel were the visible flock of God, containing His sheep. They were often led astray and scattered. But the Shepherd gathered them. "For thus saith the Lord God; Behold, I, even I, will both search my sheep, and seek them out. As a shepherd seeketh out his flock in the day that he is among his sheep that are scattered; so will I seek out my sheep, and will deliver them out of all places where they have been scattered." "I will seek that which was lost, and bring again that which was driven away, and will bind up that which was broken, and will strengthen that which was sick" (Ezek. 34: 12, 16). "Behold, the Lord God will come with strong hand, and His arm shall rule for Him: behold His reward is with Him, and His work before Him. He shall feed His flock like a shepherd: He shall gather the lambs with His arm, and carry them in His bosom, and shall gently lead those that are with young" (Isai. 40: 10). Not one of Christ's sheep shall ever perish. Jesus said, "What man of you, having a hundred sheep, if he lose one of them, doth not leave the ninety and nine in the wilderness, and go after that which is lost, until he find it? and when he hath found it, he layeth it on his shoulders, rejoicing" (Luke 15: 4; Matt. 18: 12).

In all ages "wolves" have got into the flock; even acting as pastors or shepherds. "Woe be unto the pastors that destroy and scatter the sheep of my pasture! saith Jehovah" (Jer. 23: 1-4). "Woe be to the shepherds of Israel that do feed themselves! should not the shepherds feed the flock?" "Thus saith the Lord God; Behold,

I am against the shepherds; and I will require my flock at their hand, and cause them to cease from feeding the flock" (Ezek. 34: 2-16). When Christ came, He sent forth His apostles, and commanded them, "Go not into the way of the Gentiles, and into any city of the Samaritans enter ye not: but go rather to the lost sheep of the house of Israel" (Matt. 10: 5). On another occasion, "He answered and said, I am not sent but unto the lost sheep of the house of Israel" (Matt 15: 24). He afterwards tells them, "Other sheep I have, which are not of this fold: them also I must bring, and they shall hear my voice; and there shall be one fold, and one shepherd" (John 10: 16). When His work was finished, and He was about to ascend to His throne in the heavens, He commanded His disciples to disciple all nations, and gather His sheep into other folds.

In the New Testament there are also many warnings against false shepherds. The elders of the church in Ephesus were directed to be faithful in guarding the flock committed to them. "Take heed, therefore, unto yourselves, and to all the flock, over the which the Holy Ghost hath made you bishops (or overseers), to feed the Church of God, which He hath purchased with His own blood. For I know this, that after my departing shall grievous wolves enter in among you, not sparing the flock. Also of your own selves shall men arise, speaking perverse things, to draw away disciples after them" (Acts 20: 28). Peter exhorts the elders of the churches or congregations of believers, "Feed the flock of God which is among you, taking the oversight thereof, not by constraint, but willingly; not for filthy lucre, but of a ready mind; neither as being lords over God's heritage, but being ensamples to the flock. And when the chief Shepherd shall appear, ye shall receive a crown of glory that fadeth not away" (1 Pet. 5: 1).

The teachings in the Old Testament Scriptures referring to the Lord Jesus Christ as the Great Shepherd, and to believers as His sheep, should be received and fed upon. See His leading His people like a flock, Psm. 23; 80: 1; 79: 13; Isai. 63: 11. His feeding them and care for the lambs. Isai. 40: 11, gathering His flock out of all countries; bringing them into His folds, and setting up shepherds over them to feed them. Jer. 23: 3; Ezek. 34: 11–16, 23. The prophecies that He should die for His sheep, Isai. 53, and that He was equal to the Father when smitten, give spiritual food. "Awake, O sword, against my shepherd, and against the man that is my fellow, saith Jehovah of hosts: smite the shepherd, and the sheep shall be scattered" (Zech. 13: 7). Jesus applies such passages to Himself. The night He was betrayed, "Jesus saith unto them, All ye shall be offended because of me this night: for it is written, I will smite the shepherd, and the sheep of the flock shall be scattered abroad" (Matt. 26: 31; Mark 14: 27).

When Christ sent forth the twelve apostles, He said unto them, "Behold I send you forth as sheep in the midst of wolves" (Matt. 10: 16). When He sent out the seventy, He said, "Behold I send you forth as lambs among wolves" (Luke 10: 3). He then tells them, Be ye therefore wise as serpents, and harmless as doves. But beware of men: for they will deliver you up to the councils, and they will scourge you in their synagogues; and ye shall be brought before governors and kings for my sake, for a testimony against them and the Gentiles. But when they deliver you up, take no thought how or what ye shall speak: for it shall be given you in that same hour what ye shall speak. For it is not ye that speak, but the Spirit of your Father which speaketh in you" (Matt. 10: 16). "Ye shall be hated of all men for my name sake" (Matt. 10: 22; Mark 13: 13; Luke 21: 17). "Yea, the time cometh, that whosoever killeth you will think that he doeth God service" (John 16: 2). "Woe unto you, when all men shall speak well of you! for so did their fathers to the false prophets" (Luke 6: 26). "Fear not them which kill the body, but are not able to kill the soul: but rather fear him which is able to destroy both soul and body in hell. Are not two sparrows sold for a farthing? and one of them shall not fall on the ground without your Father. But the very hairs of your head are all numbered. Fear ye not therefore, ye are of more value than many sparrows" (Matt. 10: 28). "In the world ye shall have tribulation: but be of good cheer; I have overcome the world" (John 16: 33). "Fear not, little flock, for it is your Father's good pleasure to give you the kingdom" (Luke 12: 32). "Who shall separate us from the love of Christ? shall tribulation, or distress, or persecution, or famine, or nakedness, or peril, or sword? As it is written, For Thy sake we are killed all the day long; we are accounted as sheep for the slaughter. Nay, in all these things we are more than conquerors through Him that loved us. For I am persuaded, that neither death, nor life, nor angels, nor principalities, nor powers, nor things present, nor things to come, nor height, nor depth, nor any other creature, shall be able to separate us from the love of God, which is in Christ Jesus our Lord" (Rom. 8: 36). "Many are the afflictions of the righteous: but Jehovah delivereth him out of them all" (Psm. 34: 19). "For our light affliction, which is but for a moment, worketh for us a far more exceeding weight of glory" (2 Cor. 4: 17).

"Then said Jesus unto them again, Verily, verily, I say unto you, I am the door of the sheep. All that ever came before me are thieves and robbers: but the sheep did not hear them. I am the door: by me if any man enter in, he shall be saved, and shall go in and out, and find pasture. * * * I am the good shepherd: the good shepherd giveth his life for the sheep. * * * I am the good shepherd, and know my sheep, and am known of mine. As the Father knoweth me, even so know I the Father: and I lay down my life for the sheep. And other sheep I have, which are not of this fold: them also I must bring, and they shall hear my voice; and there shall be one fold, and one shepherd. Therefore doth my Father love me, because I lay down my life, that I might take it again. No man taketh it from me, but I lay it down of myself. I have power to lay it down, and I have power to take it again. * * * My sheep hear my voice, and I know them, and they follow me: and I give unto them eternal life: and they shall never perish, and no one shall snatch them out of my hand. My Father, which hath given them unto me, is greater than all; and no one is able to snatch them out of the Father's hand. I and the Father are one" (John 10: 7, 27).

Believers in the Lord Jesus Christ rejoice that He is your Shepherd; nothing can harm you. The sheep do not keep the shepherd, but the shepherd keeps the sheep. "Behold, he that keepeth Israel shall neither slumber nor sleep. Jehovah is thy keeper: Jehovah is thy shade upon thy right hand. The sun shall not smite thee by day, nor the moon by night. Jehovah shall preserve thee from all evil: He shall preserve thy soul. Jehovah shall preserve thy going out and thy coming in from this time forth and even for evermore" (Psm. 121: 4). Your Shepherd is on the throne of the universe;

you are safe forever. You may well sing, as David did a thousand years before Christ came into the world, a song filled with the assurance of faith and the assurance of hope. "For all things are yours; whether Paul, or Apollos, or Cephas, or the world, or life, or death, or things present, or things to come; all are yours; and ye are Christ's; and Christ is God's" (1 Cor. 3: 21).

Every believer in the Lord Jesus Christ can say, "Jehovah is my Shepherd; I shall not want. He maketh me to lie down in green pastures: He leadeth me beside the still waters. He restoreth my soul: He leadeth me in the paths of righteousness for His name's sake. Yea, though I walk through the valley of the shadow of death, I will fear no evil: for Thou art with me; Thy rod and Thy staff they comfort me. Thou preparest a table before me in the presence of mine enemies: Thou anointest my head with oil; my cup runneth over. Surely goodness and mercy snall follow me all the days of my life: and I will dwell in the house of Jehovah forever" (Psalm 23).

CHRIST THE HEAD, AND BELIEVERS IN HIM MEMBERS OF HIS BODY.

THE Word of God tells us, that the Lord Jesus Christ "is the image of the invisible God, the first-born of every creature: for by Him were all things created, that are in heaven, and that are in earth, visible and invisible, whether they be thrones, or dominions, or principalities, or powers: all things were created by Him, and for him; and He is before all things, and by Him all things consist. And He is the head of the body, the Church" (Col. 1: 15; Heb. 1: 2, 3, 8). The Church is said to be the body of Christ; and every believer in Him is a particular member of the body of Christ. Paul writes to the church, in Ephesus, "I cease not to give thanks for you, making mention of you in my prayers: that the God of our Lord Jesus Christ, the Father of glory, may give unto you the spitit of wisdom and revelation in the knowledge of Him: the eyes of your understanding being enlightened, that ye may know what is the hope of His calling, and what the riches of the glory of His heritance in the saints, and what is the exceeding greatness of His power to us-ward who believe, according to the working of His mighty power, which He wrought in Christ, when He raised Him from the dead, and set Him at His own right hand in the heavenly places, far above all principality, and power, and might, and dominion, and every name that is named, not only in this world, but also in that which is to come: and hath put all things under His feet, and gave Him to be the head over all things to the church, which is His body, the fulness of Him that filleth all in all" (Eph. 1: 16).

Believers in the Lord Jesus Christ are told, "Now ye are the body of Christ, and members in particular" (1 Cor. 12: 27). "For as we have many members in one body, and all members have not the same office: so we, being many, are one body in Christ, and every one members one of another" (Rom. 12: 5). "For, as the body is one, and hath many members, and all the members of that one body, being many, are one body: so also is Christ. For by one spirit are we all baptized into one body, whether we be Jews or Gentiles, whether we be bond or free; and have been all made to drink into one spirit. For the body is not one member, but many. If the foot shall say, Because I am not the hand, I am not of the body; is it therefore not of the body? and if the ear shall say, Because I am not the eye, I am not of the body; is it therefore not of the body? If the whole body were an eye, where were the hearing? If the whole were hearing, where were the smelling? But now hath God set the members every one of them in the body, as it hath pleased Him. And if they were all one member, where were the body? But now are they many members, yet but one body. And the eye cannot say unto the hand, I have no need of thee: nor again the head to the feet, I have no need of you. Nay, much more those members of the body, which seem to be more feeble are necessary" (1 Cor. 12: 12).

Rejoice, humble believer, you who think you have only one talent, or think you have none; if you believe with your heart in the Lord Jesus Christ, you are a member of His body. Every member of His body, however insignificant in the eyes of the world, is cared for by Him. For "those members of the body which we think to be less honorable, upon these we bestow the more abundant honor; and our uncomely parts have more abundant comeliness. For our comely parts have no need: but God hath tempered the body together, having given more abundant honor to that part which lacked: that there should be no schism in the body; but that the members should have the same care one for another. And whether one member suffer, all the members suffer with it; or one member be honored, all the members rejoice with it. Now, ye are the body of Christ, and members in particular" (1 Cor. 12: 23). Believer in Christ, you are a member of "His body, of His flesh, and of His bones" (Eph. 5: 30). Nothing can touch you, or harm you, without Christ, the head of the body, instantly feeling it; nay, more, knowing beforehand of it; and He will take care of His own body. So you need not fear things present or things to come, for your Head is on the throne of the universe. "In Him dwelleth all the fulness of the Godhead bodily. And ye are complete in Him, which is the head of all principality and power" (Col. 2: 9). Christ has made provision for His body; that every member is not only cared for and protected, but that it should grow with the rest of the body. Any member of the body that does not grow is a sad sight. To promote growth, "He gave some, apostles; and some, prophets; and some, evangelists; and some, pastors and teachers; for the perfecting of the saints, unto the work of ministering, unto the building up of the body of Christ: till we all attain unto the unity of the faith, and of the knowledge of the Son of God, unto a full grown man, unto the measure of the stature of the fulness of Christ: that we may be no longer children, tossed to and fro and carried about with every wind of doctrine, by the sleight of men, in craftiness, after the wiles of error; but speaking truth in love, may grow up in all things unto Him, which is the head, even Christ; in whom all the body fitly framed and knit together through that which every joint supplieth, according to the working of each several part, maketh the increase of the body unto the building up of itself in love" (Eph. 4: 11). "Let no man therefore judge you in meat, or in drink, or in respect of a holyday, or of the new moon, or of the Sabbath days which are a shadow of things to come, but the body is of Christ. Let no man beguile you of your reward in a voluntary humility and worshipping of angels, intruding into those things which he hath not seen, vainly puffed up by his fleshly mind, and not holding the Head, from which all the body by joints and hands having nourishment ministered, and knit together, increaseth with the increase of God. Wherefore if ye be dead with Christ from the rudiments of the world, why, as though living in the world, are ye subject to ordinances (touch not; taste not; handle not; which all are to perish with the using), after the commandments and doctrines of men? Which things have indeed a shew of wisdom in will-worship and humility and neglecting of the body; not in any honor to the satisfying of the flesh " (Col. 2 : 16). The children of God need these warnings that they may not be misled by infidel teachers, idolatrous churches, or the churches that put their traditions in the place of the Word of God.

Bear in mind, the visible Church is not the body of Christ. By far the larger part of the visible Church for the last twelve hundred years has been, and now is, Antichrist. They only are members of the body of Christ, who believe His word : believe in Him and in Him alone. In His prayer when with His disciples, the night in which He was betrayed, Jesus said, "I have manifested thy name unto the men whom thou gavest me out of the world: thine they were and thou gavest them to me; and they have kept thy word; * * * sanctify them in the truth; thy word is truth. * * * Neither for these only do I pray, but for them also that shall believe on me through their word; that they may all be one; even as thou, Father, art in me, and I in thee, that they also may be in us; that the world may believe that thou didst send me. And the glory which thou hast given me I have given unto them; that they be one, even as we are one; I in them, and thou in me, that they may be perfected into one; that the world may know that thou didst send me, and lovedst them, even as thou lovedst me" (John 17: 6, 17, 20). Believer in the Lord Jesus Christ, He who uttered that prayer has all power in heaven and on earth. Receiving and believing in Him you become a child of God (John 1: 12); a member of His body. You have now an everlasting life (John 3: 36). All things are working together for your good (Rom. 8: 28); nothing can separate you from His love (Rom. 8: 39), and all things are now yours (1 Cor. 3, 22). Therefore, we are told to grow in the grace and in the knowledge of our Lord and Saviour Jesus Christ (2 Pet. 3: 18). "Grow up in all things unto him, which is the head, even Christ" (Eph. 4: 15). As a member of His body and a partaker of His Spirit; as the members of the body are guided, moved and protected by the head, so must we be continually "looking unto Jesus, the author and finisher of our faith," our Head, for life, for light, for guidance, and for protection. United to Him as members of His body, let Him work through us: and let us give Him the glory. He will not allow any member of His body to be lost. He has said, "Because I live, ye shall live also" (John 14: 19). "Be strong in the Lord and in the power of his might" (Eph. 6: 10). Say with Paul, "I can do all things through Christ which strengtheth me" (Phil. 4: 13). Members of the body of Christ "should have the same care one for another. And whether one member suffer, all the members suffer with it; or one member be honored, all the members rejoice with it. Now ye are the body of Christ, and members in particular." (1 Cor. 12: 25).

CHRIST THE VINE, BELIEVERS IN HIM THE BRANCHES.

One of the most instructive of the many illustrations in the Bible of the union of Christ and believers is that of the Vine and its branches. Christ calls Himself the true Vine; and believers in Him, the branches. It teaches that there must be a continued living union between them, that our life is in Him, and from Him; and that separated from Him there is no spiritual life, no spiritual growth, no fruit or good works that glorify God, or are acceptable to God. " Without faith it is impossible to please Him" (Heb. 11 : 6). "In Jesus Christ, neither circumcision availeth anything, nor incircumcision; but faith which worketh by love" (Gal. 5 : 6). "Whatsoever is not of faith is sin" (Rom. 14: 23). Faith in the Lord Jesus Christ will show itself in bearing fruit, in good works. "Faith without works is dead" (James 1: 17,20). By faith we accept Christ; by faith we abide in Him. He says, " Come unto me, all ye that labor and are heavy laden, and I will give you rest. Take my yoke upon you, and learn of me; for I am meek and lowly in heart, and ye shall find rest unto your souls. For my yoke is easy, and my burden is light" (Matt. 11 : 28).

When He was on earth, He told His disciples to follow Him. He now invites us not only to come to Him, and cast all our burdens, all our sins on Him; but He adds, Abide in me, and He promises to abide in us, thus making us one with Him, that we may have in Him continued life, nourishment and growth, and thus produce fruit to the glory of God. Jesus had just told His disciples that He would come with the Father and abide with them. He also promised that the Holy Spirit would abide in them. "Verily, verily, I say unto you, he that believeth on me, the works that I do shall he do also; and greater works than these shall he do; because I go unto my father. And whatsoever ye shall ask in my name, that will I do, that the Father may be glorified in the Son. If ye shall ask anything in my name, I will do it. If ye love me keep my commandments. And I will pray the Father, and he shall give you another Comforter that he may abide with you forever. * * * I will not leave you comfortless (orphans). I will come to you. Yet a little while, and the world seeth me no more, but ye see me: because I live ye shall live also. At that day ye shall know that I am in my Father, and ye in me, and I in you." * * * Judas saith unto Him, not Iscariot, Lord, how is it that Thou wilt manifest Thyself unto us, and not unto the world? Jesus answered, and said unto him, "If a man love me, he will keep my words: and my Father will love him, and we will come unto him, and make our abode with him" (John 14: 12, 18, 22). These promises depend on our coming to the Lord Jesus Christ; knowing Him, receiving Him, believing in Him, loving Him, keeping His word, keeping His commandments, and abiding in Him. Instead of thinking of a dead Christ, of a far distant Christ, of a child Christ, of a Christ on the cross as too many do, the believer can know a living, loving, everpresent Christ, who abides in him, and in whom he abides. He believes His words, "I am the true Vine, and my Father is the husbandman. Every branch in me that beareth not fruit he taketh away: and every branch that beareth fruit, he cleanseth it, that it may bear more fruit. Already ye are clean because of the word which I have spoken unto you. Abide in me, and I in you. As the branch cannot bear fruit of itself except it abide in the vine; so neither can ye, except ye abide in me. I am the Vine, ye are the branches; he that abideth in me, and I in him, the same bringeth forth much fruit: for apart from me ye can do nothing. If a man abide not in me, he is cast forth as a branch, and is withered; and men gather them, and cast them into the fire, and they are burned. If ye abide in me, and my words abide in you, ask whatsoever ye will, and it shall be done unto you. Herein is my Father glorified, that ye bear much fruit; and so shall ye be my disciples. Even as the Father hath loved me, I also have loved you: abide ye in my love. If ye keep my commandments, ye shall abide in my love; even as I have kept my Father's commandments, and abide in his love. These things have I spoken unto you, that my joy may be in you, and that your joy may be fulfilled. This is my commandment, that ye love one another, as I have loved you" (John 15: 1). Ye have not chosen me, but I have chosen you, and ordained you, that ye should go and bring forth fruit, and that your fruit should remain : that whatsoever ye shall ask of the Father in my name, he may give it to you" (John 15 : 16 ; 16: 23). "Verily, verily, I say unto you, he that believeth on me, the works that I do shall he do also; and greater works than these shall he do; because I go unto my Father. And whatsoever ye shall ask in my name, that will I do, that the Father may be glorified in the Son. If ye shall ask anything in my name, I will do it" (John 14: 12). "What ye will." "Whatsoever." "Anything." Believing in Christ, we believe His promises made to us. We can "go boldly" to the throne of grace, with the certainty of having what we ask in His name. We do not go merely as suppliants for ourselves, or as suppliants for Him ; but we have His anthority to ask in His name. "Whatsoever ye shall ask in my name, that will I do."

We must remember that these promises, again and again repeated, depend on our union with Him; drawing life from Him; partaking of

His Spirit; moved by Him; He praying through us, the Spirit helping our infirmities; for we know not what we should pray for as we ought. (Rom. 8: 26) Then it will be Christ praying through us. We shall ask only according to His will; and it will be done for us. Believing these words, the child of God looks to the Lord Jesus Christ for everything; lives moment by moment by faith in Him; draws life from Him, as the branch from the vine; feeds upon His word, and is constantly growing in spiritual strength by His Spirit working in him; and thus produces fruit to the glory of God abundantly. Paul, writing of the casting away of some of the Jews, and the introduction of the Gentiles into the church, says, "If the root is holy, so are the branches. But if some of the branches were broken off, and thou, being a wild olive, wast grafted in among them, and didst become partaker with them of the root of the fatness of the olive tree; glory not over the branches; but if thou gloriest, it is not thou that bearest the root, but the root thee." (Rom. 11: 16).

The believer may well rejoice that he is a branch of the Vine and that Jehovah is the husbandman. "The vineyard of the Lord of Hosts is the house of Israel" (Isai. 5: 7). "Thou hast brought a vine out of Egypt; * * * Return, we beseech thee, O God of Hosts look down from heaven, and behold, and visit the vine; and the vineyard which thy right hand hath planted, and the branch that thou madest strong for thyself" (Psm. 80: 8, 14). "In that day sing ye unto her, a vineyard of red wine. I the LORD do keep it; I will water it every moment: lest any hurt it, I will keep it night and day" (Isai. 27: 2). Christ says: "My Father is the husbandman. Every branch in me that beareth not fruit, He taketh away; and every branch that beareth fruit, he cleanseth it, that it may bear more fruit." "Herein is my Father glorified, that ye bear much fruit; and so shall ye be my disciples" (John 15: 1, 8).

The Parable thus teaches us another very important truth. The child of God must suffer in this life. He must be pruned that he may bear fruit. "Every branch in me that beareth not fruit, He taketh away: and every branch that beareth fruit, He purgeth it, that it may bring forth more fruit" (John 15: 2). The Psalmist wrote, "Many are the afflictions of the righteous; but the LORD delivereth him out of them all" (Psm. 34: 19). " Before I was afflicted I went astray; but now have I kept Thy word." "It is good for me that I have been afflicted, that I might learn Thy statutes." "I know, O Lord, that Thy judgments are right, and that Thou in faithfulness hast afflicted me" (Psm. 119: 67, 71, 75). The child of God can look upon the removal of loved ones, the loss of health, of property, as prunings of God for our better fruit bearing, and for His glory. Christians are made partakers of the sufferings of Christ, not only those He endured for them, but they also are to suffer for His sake. "For unto you it is given in the behalf of Christ, not only to believe on Him, but also to suffer for His sake" (Phil. 1: 29). "If we suffer, we shall also reign with Him" (2 Tim. 2: 12). "But rejoice, inasmuch as ye are partakers of Christ's sufferings; that when His glory shall be revealed, ye may be glad also with exceeding joy" (1 Pet. 4: 13). "But the God of all grace, who hath called us unto his eternal glory by Christ Jesus, after that ye have suffered a while, make you perfect, stablish, strengthen, settle you" (1 Pet. 5: 10).

As the wind shaking the tree causes it to extend its roots deeper into the soil, so afflictions to the Christian causes him to cling more closely to Christ. One of the greatest gifts of the Spirit to the Christian, producing the most precious fruit, is patience and long suffering. "That ye might walk worthy of the Lord unto all pleasing, being fruitful in every good work, and increasing in the knowledge of God; strengthened with all might, according to His glorious power, unto all patience and long suffering with joyfulness" (Col. 1: 9). "Strengthened with might by His Spirit in the inner man; that Christ may dwell in your hearts by faith; that ye, being rooted and grounded in love, * * * and to know the love of Christ, which passeth knowledge, that ye might be filled with all the fullness of God" (Eph. 3: 16). "As ye have therefore received Christ Jesus the Lord, so walk in Him; rooted and built up in Him and stablished in the faith" (Col. 2: 6).

United to Christ, as a branch is united to the vine, and having Christ and the Holy Spirit abiding in you, you can say, "I am crucified with Christ, nevertheless I live; yet not I, but Christ liveth in me: and the life which I now live in the flesh I live by the faith of the Son of God, who loved me, and gave Himself for me" (Gal. 2: 20). As a living branch in the true Vine you will bear fruit. "Herein is My Father glorified that ye bear much fruit; so shall ye be My disciples" (John 15: 8). "He that keepeth His commandments dwelleth in Him, and He in him. And hereby we know that He abideth in us by the Spirit which He had given us" (1 John 3: 24). "He that saith he abideth in Him, ought himself so to walk, even as He walked" (1 John 2: 6). "And now, little children, abide in Him; that, when He shall appear, we may have confidence, and not be ashamed before Him at His coming" (1 John 2: 28).

UNION OF BELIEVERS WITH CHRIST, AND THE HOLY SPIRIT AND THE FATHER. ONE IN GOD.

CHRIST told His disciples "Ye shall be brought before governors and kings for My sake, for a testimony against them and the Gentiles. But when they deliver you up, take no thought how or what ye shall speak; for it shall be given you in that same hour what ye shall speak. For "it is not ye that speak, but the Spirit of your Father which speaketh in you" (Matt. 10: 18). "It is not ye that speak, but the Holy Ghost" (Mark 13: 11). In His last talk with His disciples before His crucifixion He said to them that He was going to leave them for a time, and would come again; and that the Holy Spirit would come and abide with them. He said, "If ye love Me, ye will keep My commandments. And I will pray the Father, and He shall give you another Comforter, that He may be with you forever, even the Spirit of truth: whom the world cannot receive; for it beholdeth Him not, neither knoweth Him; ye know Him; for He abideth with you, and shall be in you. I will not leave you desolate (orphans); I will come unto you. Yet a little while and the world beholdeth Me no more; but ye behold Me; because I live, ye shall live also"

(John 14: 15). "The Comforter, even the Holy Spirit, whom the Father will send in My name, He shall teach you all things, and bring to your remembrance all that I said unto you" (John 14: 26). "When the Comforter is come, whom I will send unto you from the Father, even the Spirit of truth, which proceedeth from the Father, He shall bear witness of Me" (John 15: 26). "It is expedient for you that I go away; for if I go not away, the Comforter will not come unto you; but if I go, I will send Him unto you. * * * When He, the Spirit of truth, is come, He shall guide you into all truth" (John 16: 7, 13).

The believer in the Lord Jesus Christ receives the Holy Spirit to abide in him forever. In fact, he is made a believer by the Holy Spirit, and is born of the Holy Spirit. Jesus told Nicodemus, a ruler, an officer in the Church "Verily, verily, I say unto thee, except a man be born again, he cannot see the kingdom of God." "Verily, verily, I say unto thee, except a man be born of water and of the Spirit he cannot enter into the kingdom of God" (John 3: 3, 5). John writes: "As many as received Him, to them He gave the right to become children of God, even to them that believe on His name; which were born (begotten), not of blood, nor of the will of the flesh, nor of the will of man, but of God" (John 1: 12).

The Holy Spirit, dwelling in believers, produces all spiritual life. "Ye are not in the flesh, but in the Spirit, if so be the Spirit of God dwelleth in you. But if any man hath not the Spirit of Christ, he is none of His" * * * "But if the Spirit of Him that raised up Jesus from the dead dwelleth in you, He that raised up Christ Jesus from the dead shall quicken also your mortal bodies through His Spirit that dwelleth in you." * * * " For as many as are led by the Spirit of God, these are the sons of God." * * * "The Spirit Himself beareth witness with our spirit that we are children of God; and if children, then heirs; heirs of God, and joint heirs with Christ." * * * "The Spirit also helpeth our infirmity; for we know not how to pray as we ought; but the Spirit Himself maketh intercession for us with groanings which cannot be uttered; and he that searcheth the hearts knoweth what is the mind of the Spirit, because He maketh intercession for the saints according to the will of God" (Rom. 8: 9, 11, 14, 16, 26).

Christian works, or fruit, although coming through the branches from Christ, the Vine, are ascribed to the Holy Spirit. " The fruit of the Spirit is love, joy, peace, long suffering, kindness, goodness, faithfulness, meekness, temperance" (Gal. 5: 22).

Spiritual gifts are also ascribed to the Holy Spirit. "To one is given by the Spirit the word of wisdom; to another the word of knowledge by the same Spirit; to another faith by the same Spirit; to another the gifts of healing by the same Spirit; to another the working of miracles; to another prophecy; to another discerning of spirits: to another divers kinds of tongues; to another the interpretation of tongues; but all these worketh that one and the selfsame Spirit, dividing to every man severally as he will" (1 Cor. 12: 8).

Believers will remember that the Holy Spirit is not an influence of God, but is a person in the Godhead. We are to be baptized "into the name of the Father, and of the Son, and of the Holy Ghost" (Matt. 28: 19). The benediction is, "The grace of our Lord Jesus Christ, and the love of God, and the communion of the Holy Ghost be with you all. Amen." (2 r.Co 13: 14).

The Lord Jesus has told us that the Holy Ghost would personally come and dwell in us. Believers are warned, "Grieve not the Holy Spirit of God, in whom ye were sealed unto the day of redemption" (Eph. 4: 30). "Quench not the Spirit" (1 Thess. 5: 19). Unbelievers are told that, "whosoever shall blaspheme against the Holy Spirit hath never forgiveness, but is guilty of an eternal sin" (Mark 3: 29). "Whosoever shall speak against the Holy Spirit, it shall not be forgiven him, neither in this world, nor in that which is to come" (Matt. 12: 32).

The Temple, with its priesthood and ceremonial service, having served as a type, has passed away. As Christ told the woman of Samaria, "Ye shall neither in this mountain, nor yet at

Jerusalem, worship the Father. * * * God is a Spirit: and they that worship Him must worship Him in spirit and in truth" (John 4: 21, 24). Isaiah 700 years before Christ wrote, "For thus saith the high and lofty One that inhabiteth eternity, whose name is Holy; I dwell in the high and holy place, with him also that is of a contrite and humble spirit; to revive the spirit of the humble, and to revive the heart of the contrite ones" (Isai. 57: 15). Paul tells the Athenians, "God that made the world and all things therein, seeing that He is Lord of heaven and earth, dwelleth not in temples made with hands; neither is worshipped with men's hands as though He needed anything, seeing He giveth to all life, and breath, and all things. * * * for in Him we live, and more, and have our being" (Acts. 17: 24, 28). The children of God are now the temple of God; for God the Holy Ghost abides in them, "know ye not that ye are the temple of God, and that the Spirit of God dwelleth in you?" (1 Cor. 3: 16). "What! know ye not that your body is the temple of the Holy Ghost which is in you, which ye have of God, and ye are not your own? For ye are bought with a price: therefore glorify God in your body, and in your spirit, which are God's" (1 Cor. 6: 19). "Be ye not unequally yoked together with unbelievers: for what fellowship hath righteousness with unrighteousness? and what communion hath light with darkness? and what concord hath Christ with Belial? or what part hath he that believeth with an infidel? And what agreement hath the temple of God with idols? for ye are the temple of the living God; as God hath said, I will dwell in them, and walk in them; and I will be their God, and they shall be my people. Wherefore come out from among them, and be ye separate, saith the Lord, and touch not the unclean thing: and I will receive you, and will be a Father unto you, and ye shall be My sons, and daughters, saith the Lord Almighty" (2 Cor. 6: 16).

Receiving the Lord Jesus Christ, and united to Him, as the hand or foot is to the head of the body; drawing life from Him, as the branch does from the vine; and having the Holy Spirit dwelling in us, making us the temple of God; we can say "truly our fellowship is with the Father, and His Son Jesus Christ. * * * If we walk in the light, as He is in the light, we have fellowship one with another" (1 John 1: 3, 7).

Union with Christ is union with all those who believe in Christ, and who walk in the light, as He is in the light." It is not a union with infidel or idolatrous churches calling themselves Christian. The prayer of the Lord Jesus Christ has been fulfilled ever since it was uttered. "Neither pray I for these alone, but for them also which shall believe on Me through their word; that they all may be one; as thou, Father, art in me, and I in Thee, that they also may be one in us: that the world may believe that Thou hast sent Me. And the glory which

Thou gavest Me I have given them; that they may be one, even as We are one: I in them, and Thou in Me; that they may be perfect in one; and that the world may know that Thou hast sent Me, and has loved them, as Thou hast loved Me" (John 17: 20).

As a member of the body of Christ, as a branch of the Vine Christ, as the temple of the Holy Ghost, as one with Christ, with the Holy Ghost, and with the Father: the believer is one with God. Although he may, for his own eternal good, and for the glory of God, be called to suffer pain, poverty, sickness, bereavement, persecution, and bodily death; yet he knows that all these things and all other things are working together for his good; that all things present and to come are now his; and that he has now an everlasting life, which no being can take from him; for his life is hid with Christ in God. When Christ, who is our life, shall appear, then shall ye also appear with Him in glory" (Col. 3: 3). "Fear thou not, for I am with thee; be not dismayed, for I am thy God. I will strengthen thee; yea, I will help thee; yea, I will uphold thee with the right hand of My righteousness. For I, Jehovah, thy God, will hold thy right hand, saying unto thee: Fear not, I will help thee" (Isai. 41: 10, 13, 14). "When thou passest through the waters, I will be with thee; and through the rivers, they shall not overflow thee; when thou walkest through the fire, thou shalt not be burned; neither shall the flame kindle upon thee. For I am Jehovah, thy God, the Holy One of Israel, thy Saviour" (Isai. 43: 3). "He hath said, I will never leave thee, not forsake thee" (Heb. 13: 5). "Because I live, ye shall live also" (John 14: 19).

"Now the God of peace, that brought again from the dead our Lord Jesus, that great Shepherd of the sheep, through the blood of the everlasting Covenant, make you perfect in every good work to do His will, working in you that which is well pleasing in His sight, through Jesus Christ; to whom be glory for ever and ever. Amen." (Heb. 13: 20).

" Soul, then know thy full salvation,
    Rise o'er sin, and fear and care;
Joy, to find in every station
    Something still to do or bear.
Think what Spirit dwells within thee;
    Think what Father's smiles are thine;
Think that Jesus died to win thee!
    Child of God, canst thou repine?"

" Haste thee on from grace to glory,
    Armed by faith, and winged by prayer!
Heaven's eternal day's before thee,
    God's own hand shall guide thee there.
Soon shall close thy earthly mission,
    Soon shall pass thy pilgrim days,
Hope shall change to glad fruition,
    Faith to sight, and prayer to praise."

THE "I AM" OF JESUS.

Before Abraham was, I am.—John 8: 58.
I am the light of the world.—John 8: 12.
I am the door.—John 10: 7.
I am the way, the truth, and the life.—John 14: 6
I am the living bread.—John 6: 51
I am the bread of life.—John 6: 35
I am the true vine.—John 15: 1,
I am the good shepherd.—John 10: 11, 14.
I am the resurrection, and the life.—John 11: 25.
I am with you alway.—Matt. 28: 20

I am with thee.—Acts 18: 10.
There am I in the midst of them.—Matt. 18: 20.
I am Alpha and Omega, the beginning and the ending.—Rev. 1: 8.
I am the first and the last.—Rev. 1: 17.
I am from above......I am not of this world.—John 8: 23.
I am alive for evermore.—Rev. 1: 18.
I am Jesus whom thou persecutest.—Acts 9: 5.
Be with me where I am.—John 17: 24.

THE "ME" OF JESUS.

Ye believe in God, believe also in me.—John 14: 1.
All things are delivered unto me.—Matt. 11: 27.
All power is given unto me in heaven and in earth.—Matt. 28: 18.
He that hath seen me hath seen the Father.—John 14: 9.
Whosoever liveth and believeth in me shall never die.—John 11: 26.
He that believeth on me hath everlasting life.—John 6: 47.
Come unto me, all *ye* that labour and are heavy laden.—Matt. 11: 28.
Him that cometh to me I will in no wise cast out.—John vi: 37.
He that cometh to me shall never hunger.—John 6: 35.
He that believeth on me shall never thirst.—John 6: 35.
No man cometh unto the Father, but by me.—John 14: 6.
In me ye might have peace.—John 16: 33.
By me if any man enter in, he shall be saved.—John 10: 9.
Follow me.—Matt. 8: 22; 9: 9; Mark 8: 34; 10: 21.
Follow me, and I will make you fishers of men.—Matt. 4: 19.
He that followeth me shall not walk in darkness.—John 8: 12.
They follow me: and I give unto them eternal life.—John 10: 27, 28.
Abide in me, and I in you.—John 15: 4.
Ye did *it* not to me.—Matt. 25:45.

He that abideth in me, and I in him.—John 15: 5.
Without me ye can do nothing.—John 15: 5.
As thou Father, *art* in me, and I in thee.—John 17: 21.
He that eateth me, even he shall live by me.—John 6: 57.
Suffer the little children to come unto me.—Mark 10: 14.
Learn of me.—Matt. 11: 29.
Whosoever will come after me.—Mark 8: 34.
Ye have done *it* unto me.—Matt. 25: 40.
If any man serve me, let him follow me.—John 12: 26.
He that receiveth you receiveth me.—Matt. 10: 40.
He that loveth father or mother more that me.—Matt. 10: 37.
He that is not with me is against me.—Matt. 12: 30.
He that gathereth not with me scattereth.—Matt. 12: 30.
Whosoever therefore shall be ashamed of me.—Mark 8: 38.
I, if I be lifted up....will draw all men unto me.—John 12: 32.
Whosoever therefore shall confess me before men.—Matt. 10: 32.
Ye shall be witnesses unto me.—Acts 1: 8.
If a man love me, he will keep my words.—John 14: 23.
To-day shalt thou be with me in paradise.—Luke 23: 43.

GOD DWELLING IN US.

Whosoever shall confess that Jesus is the Son of God, God dwelleth in him, and he in God.—1 John 4: 15.

I will pray the Father, and he shall give you another Comforter, that he may abide with you forever; *even* the Spirit of truth; whom the world cannot receive, because it seeth him not, neither knoweth him; but ye know him; for he dwelleth with you, and shall be in you.—John 14: 16, 17.

Know ye not that ye are the temple of God, and *that* the Spirit of God dwelleth in you?—1 Cor. 3: 16.

What! know ye not that your body is the temple of the Holy Ghost, *which is* in you?—1 Cor. 6: 19.

For ye are the temple of the living God; as God hath said, I will dwell in them, and walk in *them.*—2 Cor. 6: 16.

If the Spirit of him that raised up Jesus from the dead dwell in you, he that raised up Christ from the dead shall also quicken your mortal bodies by his Spirit that dwelleth in you.—Rom. 8: 11.

And hereby we know that he abideth in us, by the Spirit which he hath given us.—1 John 3: 24.

Hereby know we that we dwell in him, and he in us; because he hath given us of his Spirit.—1 John 4: 13.

Lo, I am with you alway, *even* unto the end of the world.—Matt. 28: 20.

As thou Father, *art* in me, and I in thee, that they also may be one in us.—John 17: 21. I in them, and thou in me.—John 17: 23. That the love wherewith thou hast loved me may be in them, and I in them.—John 17: 26.

I *am* in my Father; and ye in me, and I in you.—John 14: 20.

If a man love me, he will keep my words: and my Father will love him, and we will come unto him, and make our abode with him.—John 14: 23.

BELIEVERS SAVED.

He that believeth on me hath everlasting life.—John 6: 47. I give unto them eternal life; and they shall never perish.—John 10: 28. Because I live, ye shall live also.—John 14: 19.

He that believeth on the Son hath everlasting life.—John 3: 36. And shall not come into condemnation; but is passed from death unto life.—John 5: 24.

Whosoever believeth that Jesus is the Christ is born of God.—1 John 5: 1. Beloved, now are we the sons of God.—1 John 3: 2. We know that we have passed from death unto life.—1 John 3: 14.

And this is the record, that God hath given to us eternal life. These things have I written unto you that believe on the name of the Son of God; that ye may know that ye have eternal life.—1 John 5: 11, 13.

Giving thanks unto the Father, which hath made us meet to be partakers of the inheritance of the saints in light; who hath delivered us from the power of darkness, and hath translated *us* into the kingdom of his dear Son; in whom we have redemption through his blood, *even the* forgiveness of sins.—Col. 1: 12-14. See Rom. 8: 1, 38, 39; 5: 1.

www.ingramcontent.com/pod-product-compliance
Lightning Source LLC
Chambersburg PA
CBHW021404230426
43666CB00006B/634